# THERAPEUTIC PARENTING ESSENTIALS

# THERAPEUTIC PARENTING ESSENTIALS

## MOVING FROM TRAUMA TO TRUST

**SARAH NAISH,
SARAH DILLON and JANE MITCHELL**

Jessica Kingsley *Publishers*
London and Philadelphia

First published in 2020
by Jessica Kingsley Publishers
73 Collier Street
London N1 9BE, UK
and
400 Market Street, Suite 400
Philadelphia, PA 19106, USA

*www.jkp.com*

**Library of Congress Cataloging in Publication Data**
A CIP catalog record for this book is available from the Library of Congress

**British Library Cataloguing in Publication Data**
A CIP catalogue record for this book is available from the British Library

ISBN 978 1 78775 031 9
eISBN 978 1 78775 032 6

Printed and bound in Great Britain

# Contents

# About This Book

## Who is the book for?

**Sarah Naish:** The purpose of this story is to help *all* parents who are raising children who have experienced trauma.

It helps to assure us all that we are not alone and that our stories CAN and often DO have a positive ending, despite the challenges.

After the success of my last book, *The A–Z of Therapeutic Parenting*, many parents asked me how I had managed to raise my five adopted children and stay so grounded! After some reflection I realised that I had not always been grounded. In fact, the early years with the children were quite lacking in therapeutic parenting and were much more based in the 'flying by the seat of my pants' parenting style!

The *A–Z* was written to give parents understanding about why our children do the things they do, and how we can respond to change behaviours. The one thing it didn't do was explore the EXPERIENCE of therapeutic parenting and how it FEELS. Our children's behaviour impacts on us. There is no getting away from that.

Through carefully kept diary records I have reflected on how I felt and experienced the daily challenges, which were many and complex. I believe that if parents are able to read about the experiences of other parents who have shared the same feelings about their children and behaviours, it will help us to be more open – in particular, open to hearing about our children's perspectives and understanding their feelings.

So, if you are looking after a child who has suffered from trauma and/or interrupted attachments and sometimes feel at the end of your tether, I am sure you will identify with the myriad situations we explore here together.

This book has also been written for supporters – to help them gain insight into life with a traumatised child, and to develop some knowledge and understanding of the reasons behind the behaviours the children show.

## What is therapeutic parenting?

Therapeutic parenting is a term commonly used for foster parents, adopters, special guardians and kinship carers who are looking after children who may have suffered trauma. This may be through early-life neglect and/or abuse.

Therapeutic parenting is also used by biological parents, particularly where there may have been pre-birth trauma, separation, illness, domestic violence or any other factor affecting the child's functioning and understanding of the world, or their attachment relationships. Many biological parents also find therapeutic parenting styles useful to use with children who are on the autism spectrum or have high cortisol levels and/or attention deficit hyperactivity disorder (ADHD).

Therapeutic parenting is beneficial for *all* children due to its reliance on firm boundaries and structure with a strong empathic and nurturing approach.

# About the Authors

This book is written collaboratively by three co-authors; so, before we start, let's do some introductions:

**Sarah Naish:** I am an adopter of five siblings, who are referred to in this book as Rosie, Katie, William, Sophie and Charley. I'm a former foster parent, social worker and owner of an Ofsted 'Outstanding' Independent Fostering Agency. I work full time in training and consultancy within adoption and fostering and am also the CEO of the National Association of Therapeutic Parents.

The accounts I have written within this story are an honest, no-holds-barred account of my experiences of parenting and the system which adoption and fostering is a part of. I understand that system and the impact on parents, children and supporting professionals.

**Sarah Dillon:** I am an attachment therapist, trainer, therapeutic lead for the National Association of Therapeutic Parents, and a former child in care. I write from the viewpoint of the child. I have never lost the voice of the child, and aim to help us all to see every event directly through the eyes of the child.

**Jane Mitchell:** I am a birth mother to three children (now grown up!) and also an adopter. I specialise in developing resources and training around attachment, developmental trauma and related neuroscience. I'm co-author of the Diploma in Therapeutic Parenting and the accompanying handbook for the Diploma, *The Complete Guide to Therapeutic*  *Parenting*. I have worked with adoptive and foster families for over 15 years and am also a founding committee member of the National Association of Therapeutic Parents.

## How this book is written

This book is written collaboratively in order to highlight two important perspectives – that of the parent, and that of the child.

**Sarah Naish** writes from her direct experiences as an adoptive parent. She describes her feelings upon meeting her children and throughout the difficulties (and joys) experienced during the children's childhood before arriving at a position of family stability many years later.

**Sarah Dillon** draws on her own lived childhood experiences to write in the voice of Sarah's children: Rosie, Katie, William, Sophie and Charley. Their story begins as they were taken into care, and we then follow them through their life-changing moments, fear-based behaviours and finally as they develop trust, ending in a stable family unit.

Throughout the writing of this book, Sarah Dillon has worked closely with now-adult Rosie to ensure that her portrayal of the children's voices is authentic. Their experiences within the care system were remarkably similar and it is this shared experience that has enabled Sarah to write from the perspective of the children.

**Jane Mitchell** provides the commentary on the story as it unfolds. She draws on her professional and personal expertise to explain what's really going on in the family's interactions, including the often-conflicting viewpoints of the therapeutic parent and their child. As well as helping to make sense of the scenarios, the commentaries are accompanied by points for reflection and tips for you to try at home. Jane has also created Appendices, where you can find out more about some of the theories which are talked about in this book, and a Glossary providing definitions of words that may be unfamiliar.

Both Jane Mitchell and Sarah Dillon know Sarah Naish's (now adult) children and work alongside two of them professionally. We have taken great care to ensure that the views, thoughts and feelings attributed to them in our books are authentic.

# Introduction

When we begin our journey to family, either as the parent or child, none of us realise quite how bumpy the road might be. Before you hear about Sarah Naish's own story, here is a useful analogy devised by Sarah Dillon which we'll return to throughout the book. It gives a wonderful, clear explanation about how trauma affects our children and creates a backdrop against which we will set our story.

## The trauma difference

Imagine two rooms separated only by a paper-thin wall.

## Room 1

Room 1 represents the trauma history of the child. What might we find in Room 1?

- Unmet basic needs (neglect)

- Domestic abuse

- Addictions

- Scapegoating

- Violence

- Chaos

- Ignoring

- Screaming, shouting, swearing

- Abandonment and rejection

- Unavailable adults

- Unsafe and/or terrifying adults

- Unmet educational needs

- Unmet medical needs

- Isolation

- No play or adult interaction

- Wee and poo issues (if not potty trained)

- No co-regulation[1]

- No predictability

- No routines

- No boundaries

- No affection

- Sexual abuse

- Physical abuse

- Emotional and psychological abuse

- Lack of food/incorrect food

- Lack of toilet training

---

1   Co-regulation occurs, for example, when the parent is attuned to the child's distress and responds in a way that soothes the child; as the child becomes calm, the parent's anxiety is reduced in turn.

- Not weaned properly

- No fun, no day trips or holidays

- No one attending to child at night

- Threats

- Dangerous animals

- Hygiene needs not met

- Lack of medical care

- No clean clothes

- No dentist

- Inappropriate access to internet, phones and games

In Room 1, ALL adults are unsafe and won't or can't meet the child's needs. In Room 1, all you can do is survive and STAY ALIVE.

## Room 2

Room 2 is where the child lives now, with safe reliable parents. What might we find in Room 2?

- Warmth, care, love

- Predictability

- Stability

- Food

- Boundaries

- Routine

- Nurture

- Parental engagement and supervision

- Play

- Needs met

- Safe and available adults

- Acceptance

- Predictability

- Affection

- Structure

- Educational and medical needs met

- Fun, day trips and holidays

- Clean clothes and bed

- Toys and appropriate games

- Hygiene

- Medical needs met

- Dentist

In Room 2, adults are safe and will meet your needs. In Room 2, a child will THRIVE. We would all agree that every child should be born into Room 2.

Most brain development happens post-natally (i.e. after the child is born). Important neurological pathways are built when a child feels safe enough to attach to a responsive and available caregiver who consistently meets their needs between the ages of 0 and 3 years. During this time 1,000 cells per second develop in the baby's brain (see for example research by Bruce Perry and Daniel Siegel). When their needs are not met, the child will develop maladaptive attachment behaviour in order to have their needs met, and to stay alive. For example, a child that is consistently ignored will do whatever they can to get the attention of the parent because their survival depends on it – so as their distress increases they will scream and cry and thrash around. Further to this, the child is conditioned to believe that what happened in Room 1 is normal and is how ALL adults behave.

## Porous walls

Unfortunately, there is only a paper-thin wall separating Room 1 and Room 2. The wall is porous too, so experiences and memories from Room 1 seep through these pores into Room 2.

What might this metaphor look like in real life, in a family setting? Throughout our story you will see multiple examples of past-life trauma impacting on our family's present life. For example:

- A child might recreate the literal chaos of Room 1 in their own bedroom.

- A child may have wee and poo issues due to not being potty trained or as a communication of abuse and other trauma.

- If the child has lived with domestic abuse, they may well befriend the parent/caregiver in Room 2 that they perceive as the inevitable perpetrator.

- The child may reject the main caregiver as an unsafe adult.

By experiencing repeated negative actions in Room 1, a child can become conditioned, so they only feel comfortable behaving in this way. They go on to stimulate the same environment in Room 2 (e.g. behaving in controlling ways) to elicit the same response.

They *unconsciously* recreate the chaos of Room 1 in Room 2. This could involve pushing the safe parent's buttons to get that parent to reject them, hit them, take their possessions, abuse them, ground them, scream, shout or swear at them. They may also scapegoat another child in the house.

## The trap door

Room 2 not only has paper-thin walls through which trauma seeps – there is also a trap door.

The child can fall through the trap door at any time and land straight back into Room 1 – emotionally, psychologically and on a sensory or visceral level – even though their body is still in Room 2.

The trap door can be triggered by something known or unknown in Room 2 which leads them to re-experience something historical in the here and now. The child experiences this as if it's actually happening again! Examples of this will be given in Chapter 10, 'When Things Get Stuck', where we look at those times where behaviours seem to come from nowhere!

In addition, a new trigger – which can be any event which provokes a stress response in the child, such as a change to routine, an unfamiliar face or a very busy environment – can result in the child recreating actual historical events in the present. It can also lead to allegations against the 'safe parent' where the child re-experiences a traumatic experience as if it were happening now.

Finally, the child may subconsciously draw or pull the safe parent through the trap door into Room 1, where the parent quickly finds themselves reacting and behaving in ways they wouldn't normally.

## 🐾 TRY THIS...

- ✓ Try to use these useful phrases to help you 'depersonalise' your child's behaviours:

  - Child: 'It's not ME; it's what HAPPENED to me.'

  - Child: 'It's not YOU; it's what I've been through.'

  - Remember: 'An unmet need remains unmet until it's met.'

# Meet the family!

In order to give the reader a clear understanding of the members of the family that feature throughout the book, we have provided a quick-reference table below, which you can refer back to if necessary.

| Name | Who are they? | Family history |
|------|---------------|----------------|
| Sarah Naish | Adoptive mother of all five children. | Adopted William, Sophie and Charley first, then Rosie and Katie 18 months later. |
| Peter | Adoptive father of William, Sophie and Charley. | Left adoptive family one year after Rosie and Katie joined the family. |
| Ray | Step-father to all the children. | Joined the family when the children were aged between 8 and 14 years. |
| Rosie | Eldest of all the children. Very independent. | Joined adoptive family at the age of 8 years. |
| Katie | Second eldest. Very anxious as a child. | Joined adoptive family at the age of 6 years. |
| William | Middle child and the only boy. Very anxious, fearful and traumatised from experiences. | Joined adoptive family at the age of 3 years. |
| Sophie | Second youngest girl. Very compliant and charming with deep-seated, hidden issues. | Joined adoptive family at the age of 2 years. |
| Charley | Youngest child. Very controlling as a child with deep-seated attachment issues. | Joined adoptive family at the age of 7 months. |
| Jackie | Birth mother of all the children. | All children removed between the ages of 0 and 6 years, with no contact following adoption. |
| Kevin | Birth father of all the children. | All children removed with no contact following adoption. |

# 1

# **Before**

Where it all begins: there is always a beginning. A moment when a parent says, 'Could we...?', 'Should we...?' Then we take the plunge, contact the Local Authority or agency and start the process, with great expectations, trepidation and excitement.

There is also, however, a beginning for the *children*. This is often not so positive. The children are already experiencing being taken into care, then subsequently being separated into new foster families. It's a lot to bear.

### ✎ SARAH NAISH: Assessed to be a parent!

So, we are going to be assessed to see if we are worthy to be parents! Ironic really – after all this time looking after other people's children and thinking of myself as something of an expert, I am now embarking on this very long process to demonstrate to others that I can actually do it.

I don't think they realise how much I already know. I have tried to tell them, but the social worker just says, 'It's different.' Peter has already raised birth children and doesn't really want to bother with the assessment process. I think he is finding it a bit arduous.

It's taken me 15 years to accept that I won't be able to have my own biological children – 15 years of people making trite remarks such as, 'You can always adopt!', like it's equivalent to popping down to the pet shop to choose a hamster or something. They don't know the years of thought, effort, heartache and planning that have gone into making this choice. Then once the decision is made, you have to start really proving yourself.

I honestly thought that, with my background, Social Services would have been straight round asking me to sign on the dotted line, but it's actually been a long and drawn-out process. I am not convinced that the social workers communicate properly as we have had lots of duplicate forms and information.

The preparation course was quite interesting, but the only people I really wanted to talk to were the adopters and foster parents. It seemed like they had had a particularly hard time. I am pretty confident it won't be like that for us as I know all about childcare. I think they must have been very unlucky, to be honest.

I did suggest to one of the parents about using reward charts, but she just smiled at me. Maybe she didn't hear me.

Next week we are starting the part of the assessment which looks at our support. We have to do something called an Eco Map where you draw your social support structure. I am looking forward to this as I have a best friend who works in a nursery and will be brilliant. I am sure the social worker will be impressed by that. Also, my parents have said they will help out with babysitting and my other friend, Lucy, is expecting a baby next year. It will be great as we will be able to help each other out.

We have decided we would like to adopt two children – preferably girls. I am not great with babies, so my ideal would be a 2-year-old and a 4-year-old. We have our Panel date set up for six weeks' time.

It's so exciting!

## Removal

Rosie, Katie, William and Sophie were removed from their birth parents, Kevin and Jackie, when they were aged 6, 3 and 2 years, and 18 months, respectively. The children had suffered extreme neglect and abuse since their birth, and other children had died in the birth family. Charley was born while her older siblings were in foster care, and she joined Sophie and William in their foster family.

## GOING INTO CARE (Rosie, 5 years)

*The social worker's here again.*
*We're going into care.*
*Jackie hates social workers,*
*Kevin starts to swear.*
*What about the others?*
*Will we stay together?*
*Are we coming back tomorrow?*
*Or will we go forever?*
*I feel sick to my stomach.*
*My head starts to hurt.*
*Tears sting my eyes,*
*Then roll down my T-shirt.*
*We don't have time to pack.*
*She says, 'We must leave now,*
*The foster carer's waiting.'*
*I hate this ugly cow*
*What does 'foster carer' mean?*
*I slump into the car.*
*Do the carers live nearby?*
*Are we travelling far?*
*Will I go to school tomorrow?*
*I love the breakfast club.*

*Where will I sleep tonight?*
*Jackie'll be down the pub.*
*So many questions*
*Flying around my head.*
*Who will feed the dog?*
*What if he ends up dead?*

## MOVING AGAIN (Rosie, 6 years)

*Moving to another placement 'cos they've had enough of us.*
*This will be our second one, and now there's such a fuss.*
*Jean and Mark say we're a handful, far too much for them to manage.*
*We need different foster carers, ones who'll help repair the 'damage'.*
*Why can't they just be honest, tell us what we know is true?*
*'Get out of our house, you nasty kids, we never wanted you!'*
*So now they're getting rid of us, they just want us gone.*
*All they ever talk about are the things that we've done wrong.*

*I'm scared to meet these other people. I don't even know their names.*
*I hope they've got a lot of food and let me play their games.*
*Will I have to change my school, or will I start another?*
*What about my sister – where's she going with my brother?*
*I'll keep my head down 'til I know how I can get on top.*
*Then I'll show them who I am and I'll be hard to stop!*
*I'm petrified of moving on but I won't let it show.*
*I'll pretend I'm strong and act not bothered when I go.*
*Hold my feelings in my chest when Jean helps pack my bag.*
*(No one ever notices when I am feeling sad.)*
*The social worker said that she'd be here at half past three.*
*I need to know what's happening. Has she forgotten me?*

*Our bags are in the hallway and Jean says that she's sorry.*
*Do I want an ice cream or a strawberry-flavoured lolly?*
*She tells us not to worry and she'll try to keep in touch.*
*Mark stays in the kitchen as he doesn't like the fuss.*
*I breathe in very deeply and put my armour on.*
*I can't show the others that I'll be sad when they are gone.*
*Gone to different families where we can 'really settle'.*
*(She made it sound so simple, like switching on the kettle.)*
*I know they'll be disappointed when I actually arrive.*
*Doing what I always do. Trying to stay alive!*

## WHAT'S HAPPENING HERE?

We can see Sarah's confidence and excitement. She feels that she has the necessary skills and knowledge. She believes that this will be an opportunity to bond with her friend who is having a baby. They will be able to compare notes! And of course, her family is so supportive! What could possibly go wrong?

Peter also believes that his experience of raising birth children is sufficient proof of his ability to parent. There is no understanding yet of what challenges might lie ahead.

It is clear that there is no real understanding of quite how profoundly a child will be affected by their early experiences from the prospective parent's point of view.

Sarah and Rosie's accounts above are coming from wildly different perspectives. We can see a glimpse from Rosie at the layers of hurt and anger, and an expectation that the next foster family will also break down as soon as the parents discover the awful truth – as the child sees it. On top of this, it looks like the children are now being separated: Rosie and Katie to one family, William and Sophie to another. This is likely to compound the children's sense of loss and make it even more difficult for them to start to trust the adults in their lives. The children are all young and may well be difficult for one set of foster parents to manage.

## ⚙ THINK...

✓ All children who enter the care system will have suffered trauma.

- How might they be feeling?

- Are they likely to feel the same way as you do about being in a family?

- What might help them on this journey?

## ✎ SARAH NAISH: Panel

When Peter and I went to Panel, we were approved for five children. This was very unusual but it happened because the social worker was aware, and had made us aware, of a sibling group of five.

Although we were approved for all five children, we were then matched only with the youngest three. At the time William (3 years) Sophie (2 years) and Charley (newborn) were with one foster family, while Rosie (7 years) and Katie (5 years) were with another. The children were seeing each other regularly.

No one felt it would be possible, either practically or emotionally, to meet all the children's competing and complex needs in one family. So, the decision was made to separate them.

# 2

# **Expectations**

In this chapter we will see the very different feelings of the prospective parents and the children, as they move closer to forming a family. The gap appears to be widening. How can this be?

So often, the parents who are excited about becoming a family are not in the right place to hear the words of caution from social workers. At the same time, the expectations of the children are filled with fear. They cannot imagine what is going to happen to them.

What does 'family' mean to Rosie, Katie, William, Sophie and Charley?

## ✎ SARAH NAISH: Anticipation

When the social worker leaves, I sit and gaze at the pictures of the children she has left with me. Originally, we had thought about adopting two little girls but now we are looking at three!

Sisters Charley (6 months) and Sophie (2 years), and their brother William (3 years). They have two older sisters, Rosie and Katie, but I don't think five children would be feasible. We only have a three-bedroom house. I think Social Services believe that because I have also worked as a social worker I can cope with anything! Our assessor has explained that the children have suffered so much trauma that they will have to be separated and they have already been put in two different foster families. Our three are in one home and the older girls (Rosie and Katie) are in another.

That's very sad.

I imagine I might be looking at these pictures in the same way that a biological parent stares at the image of a pre-natal scan. It has been a very long journey to get to this point.

I sit and dream about the way these children will fit into our family. How everyone else will interact together. How lovely it will be for my parents to have grandchildren at last!

Of course, I know that at the beginning it's bound to be a bit difficult. The children will be confused and frightened and might be suspicious of Peter and me. I know we can overcome all of this as a family. After all, we've got good experience and we know what we're doing. Peter has worked loads in a children's home too, so that will definitely help.

I wonder if the children will keep seeing each other. I am sure they will need to. That will be strange.

Sometimes I think the social worker doesn't have any faith in us, because she always seems to be warning us about the difficulties that lie ahead. It is really negative, and I've decided to more or less ignore it as it's almost like she's trying to put me off. Doesn't she realise that I have enough love and hope for everyone? I know that this is something I can do. I've worked with enough families in my social work practice. I do understand about neglect and abuse, after all. She has reminded me that the scale of the neglect and abuse is 'on a different level'. I can see that, and I know we will have our work cut out, but I am feeling confident.

I am looking forward to making a bond with my children, helping them to feel that they are worthwhile and valued. I've bought lots of new clothes already and we are planning a holiday in the next few months to help them to make up for some of the things they've lost. It's been wonderful getting all the stuff to decorate the nursery and bedrooms! I'm so full of excitement and enthusiasm for the task that lies ahead. My heart is full of hope and joy.

I let my mind drift and I think about Christmas. They are likely to move in about a month before Christmas so that will work out brilliantly. The pleasure of buying presents and seeing our children experience Christmas in a positive way. In the summer we can all go on picnics together and enjoy the long summer holidays. This really is a new start and a new family, and I am just so excited.

I think Peter is really excited too, but he isn't showing it. I think he humours me, but he's been really great doing all the decorating.

## ⌘ SOPHIE'S PINK BLANKET (Sophie, 2 years)

*I'm going to be adopted. What does this mean?*
*A forever family, a new mum, a new dad.*
*I'm scared.*
*I'm terrified.*
*What if they hurt me, don't want me, won't feed me?*
*I need my pink blanket.*
*I've already had two mums and one dad.*
*I don't want to remember my first mum – they took me away.*
*I remember her voice somewhere in my body.*
*It's not a nice feeling.*
*I can hear raised voices in my head, slamming doors.*
*I'm scared.*
*I'm terrified.*
*I need my pink blanket.*
*I know my foster mum.*
*I like her but I don't trust her.*

*I watch her closely.*

*She is very, very busy.*

*She is making me leave.*

*Perhaps she doesn't want me either.*

*I don't blame her. I'm bad, very bad.*

*I'm angry, very angry.*

*What is a forever family?*

*Will they keep me safe?*

*I need my pink blanket.*

*I don't sleep at night, the tumbles in my tummy keeps
    me awake.*

*Will someone come in the night when I cry?*

*I like the smell of my foster mum.*

*What will my new mum smell like?*

*Will I be warm? Will there be other children?*

*What if they realise how bad I am and don't want me?*

*What if they forget about my sisters?*

*I haven't seen them for ages.*

*I hope they let me bring my pink blanket.*

*I hope they let me bring my sister and brother.*

## WHAT'S HAPPENING HERE?

It is so easy to see the very different perspectives from these two equally heart-rending accounts – but this is where the divide can sometimes start.

Sarah is not thinking about the children's experience at all, but about her own hopes and dreams for the future, which is rosy and built on the childhood that she experienced, or maybe the childhood she wished she had. She knows she is safe, loving, reliable and predictable – this forms her 'internal working model' – a technical term which means her sense of who she is, and what she is capable of (for a more detailed explanation, see Appendix 1).

She has faith in her experiences, background and training. This is going to be great!

Sophie and her siblings, however, have had experiences of a different nature, and this has activated different areas of the brain. Sophie's internal working model is that she is unlovable, unworthy, unsafe. Adults are dangerous. Maybe they hurt you. And they are certainly not reliable or loving.

Sophie's experiences will not allow her to accept this huge change. Her trauma has shaped the way she sees the world. She has already been separated from her older sisters and is moving with her brother and younger sister. But can she trust the adults to organise this?

Sophie has no sense she will be looked after and wanted, never mind loved. The only anchor and safe place in her little life is her pink blanket. Her pink blanket does not ask questions; it comforts her and never lets her down.

As two worlds collide, like an irresistible force meeting an immoveable object, we will see how this story progresses. The parents and children may well struggle, due to such differences in their expectations.

## 💡 THINK...

- ✓ Think about your own childhood and then compare this to your child's. Did you have predictability? Was there a safe adult who could meet your needs?

- ✓ You will need to take the lead to help them develop new ways of managing the uncertainty and fear that they are bound to be feeling, and this will take time.

# 3

# **Meeting**

In this chapter we look at the completely different perspectives of the parent and children on meeting. There are powerful emotions involved and they fuel very different expectations of the future.

✎ SARAH NAISH: I met my children today!

What a happy day! After so long – planning, staring hard at the photographs of the children and imagining what they are like – we actually met!

It was very emotional after waiting so long to meet them. Having seen them on a video and read all that they have been through, I expected them to be much more suspicious and withdrawn, but they weren't!

We went to the current foster parent's home. The children have been living there for the last year, since they were removed from their birth parents. Sophie, William and Charley are BEAUTIFUL. After a bit of hiding, William looked at me with a big beaming smile and said, 'Mummy.' The foster parent said he had not said that before so that must be a sign! It was like he recognised me.

Sophie is a beautiful little girl. She also hid for a while and had a small tantrum but finally beamed at us both happily.

Then she allowed me to cuddle her, which was wonderful. She is 2 years and 8 months old. She isn't talking yet as she had such a bad start. The foster parent told me that when the children arrived they were terrified of the bathroom and didn't recognise cutlery.

The baby, Charley, is only 7 months old and came straight to the foster parent from hospital. She is beautiful too and I can't begin to explain what a miracle it felt to hold this little girl in my arms and see her looking up at me so trustingly. She has been with the foster parent since the day she was born, so it's truly lovely to know that she has not suffered and is likely to be completely fine.

I could see the wariness in William's eyes, which is totally understandable, but hopefully as he meets us more often, he will learn to trust us. He definitely has some delay and hardly speaks at all. He just says 'Eah' for Sophie. He is 3 years and 8 months old so he certainly has some catching up to do. He was much more wary of Peter, but Peter did manage to get Sophie and William playing horses with him!

I know there will be challenges ahead but to finally meet my children after years of longing to be 'a mummy' is emotional beyond words.

We are going to see them every day, gradually extending the time. Then we can bring them home in three weeks!

Wonderful, wonderful days!


## MEETING YOU (Sophie, 2 years and 8 months)

*I hide under the table.*
*I sit quietly in the corner.*
*Watching, just watching.*
*I'm scared.*

*I'm wobbly everywhere.*
*I cling on to my foster mum. Everyone is looking at me.*
*She tries to get me to talk to you, look at you, smile at you,*
*My 'new mummy and daddy'.*
*I can't, I don't want to, I want you to go.*
*Teletubbies is on in a minute. I might miss it.*
*There are strangers here.*
*I'm hungry, I'm always hungry. Food is my friend.*
*I cry, I throw myself on the floor and arch my back.*
*I know you're watching me. I feel your eyes, I hear your voice.*
*Maybe you will go if I do some loud screaming.*
*You won't want me then.*
*I'm scared.*
*I'm wobbly everywhere.*
*I rock, I suck my thumb.*
*I won't let anyone comfort me.*
*I hear them reassure you that I'll be fine.*
*I won't be fine, I am melting.*
*I block out the voices in the room.*
*I retreat inside my head. I feel a hand on my shoulder.*
*I stiffen.*
*I'm scared.*
*I'm wobbly everywhere.*
*I've always felt this way.*

*I know!*
*I'll smile at you so you don't kill me.*
*I'll join in your games.*
*I'll watch you to make sure I know where you are.*
*I'll keep an eye on the door.*
*And smile some more.*

## WHAT'S HAPPENING HERE?

It is so poignant to see these two points of view in close juxta-position. In the above hugely emotive pieces of writing, we can see very clearly the powerful disconnect between the parent and child at this point.

Of course, Mum is seeing exactly what she wants to see: trusting, sweet, cuddly little ones; there's just a little touch of wariness from William and a small tantrum from Sophie – well, of course, it's understandable, given what they have been through.

BUT, we know that these differences arise from completely different understandings of the world and expectations – the internal working model (see Appendix 1). So, while Mum knows absolutely that she holds the key which will unlock her own future after years of waiting – she will rescue these beautiful children who just need to be loved – the children are in a place of sheer terror. Their expectation of the adults is that they will bring pain and neglect and *hunger* – the vulnerability is absolute.

What about the baby? Sweet and innocent, no harm done there then...except that high levels of maternal cortisol (the stress hormone in the mother's bloodstream) will have damaged the foetus's brain, as will the cigarettes, alcohol or drugs. We cannot underestimate the effect of damage sustained *in utero* (in the womb).

## ☀ THINK...

- ✓ How would you feel if you were approached by a total stranger, who told you that they were your new 'mum' or 'dad'?

- ✓ How would you feel if you were encouraged to cuddle these people?

✓ Might you wonder that if you were not 'good' you might be hurt?

✓ Might you wonder what you would have to do to please these parents and stop them hurting you?

✓ How might you modify your approach when meeting your new family?

✓ Do you believe that very tiny babies will have suffered no damage?

# 4

# Moving In

Three weeks later, after tiring but exciting introductions, we see below confident and excited parents, eager to get everything right but not really noticing small signs that all is not as it seems and that there may be troubled waters ahead.

The youngest three children, William, Sophie and Charley, are now ready to move in with their forever family, but who has decided whether or not they are actually ready?

We can glimpse the beginnings of the way that misconceptions and different perceptions can develop from the very start.

## ✎ SARAH NAISH: Our children came home today

After three weeks of very intense introductions, with lots of driving, our children came home. We have been preparing for this moment for 15 years. I know Peter has already had children, but he seemed as genuinely excited as me!

The children were enthusiastic about coming home. It was a bit odd as when we left the foster parent's house they just waved goodbye and appeared fine. They have been there for nearly a year, so I would have thought they might have been more distressed – we were certainly ready for that!

I really felt for their foster mum. She was lovely and obviously loved the children. She was very brave and did not let them see her cry.

During the introductions the children have visited us and had tea at home but now they are actually here. They are asleep in the bedrooms we have prepared for them. Charley has a Winnie the Pooh nursery. Sophie and William are sharing their newly decorated room as the social worker felt that would be best. I thought it would be difficult to get them settled but they seem absolutely exhausted and went to sleep straight after their story.

The clothes we have bought them are miles too big. The foster mum did warn me about that. When she visited last week and saw their new pyjamas she explained that both William and Sophie are in age 12–18 months clothes. A lot of people take them to be twins.

I have two weeks to try to integrate the children with our three small dogs as the social workers have said William and Sophie are very fearful of all dogs. I don't want the children to go through life being scared of something that is so hard to avoid, so I am determined to make this work. I have put gates upstairs to keep them separated, so they can all get used to hearing each other. They are definitely very frightened of the dogs and need lots of reassurance.

I have tried not to go over the top buying new clothes as I know it's important to keep the children in familiar clothes. We have bought the same washing powder as the foster home's. There does seem to be a lot of washing already!

*Footnote:* 10.30 pm. I spoke too soon! William has been awake since 8.30 pm and seems unable to settle. Lots of cuddles and encouragement needed. He is worried about their older sisters, Katie and Rosie, I think. His speech is non-existent but he was holding a picture of them. It's so hard for them all to be apart.

## ♋ FOREVER FAMILY (William, 3 years)

*Off to my forever family,*
*But I've already had two.*
*A birth family, foster home,*
*And now there's you.*

*Two broken families*
*Before you bring me home*
*No one really wants me,*
*Fear in every bone.*

*I need to keep watch,*
*Must be in control,*
*Although I look so normal*
*My brain feels less than whole.*

*I'll come to you in nappies,*
*A bottle in my bag,*
*Giving you a fake smile,*
*Inside I feel so sad.*

*I know that you won't keep me,*
*I'll soon be moving on.*
*I truly can't believe you*
*When you say that you're my mum.*

*Flooded with fuzzy feelings,*
*I cannot fall to sleep.*
*I'm petrified you'll leave me.*
*This terror runs so deep.*

*When you try to soothe me,*
*I'm filled with violent rage.*
*I'll shock you with the strength I have*
*For someone of my age.*

*I know I disappoint you,*
*I see it in your eyes.*
*They told you I was perfect*
*But they were telling lies.*

*I cannot let you near me,*
*I do not trust you'll stay,*
*I'll just keep my distance*
*'Til you send me on my way.*

*Deep within my birth mum's womb,*
*Rejection filled my heart.*
*I knew I wasn't worthy*
*Right from the very start.*

*So even though you tell me*
*I'm staying here with you,*
*That hasn't been my story,*
*So, I don't feel it's true.*

## ⌘ GONE (Rosie, 7 years)

They have moved William, Sophie and Charley to a 'forever family'. Well I am glad they finally told me that because when they cancelled our visit I thought Kevin had got them.

I didn't know if they were OK. I thought they might be dead. I won't believe they are OK until I see them. I don't know where they are. Where are they?

They will miss me. I am the big sister. They need me to look after them. What if the forever family's horrible to them? They are bound to hurt them. Grown-ups always do. I'll kill them if they hurt them. What if they kill me though?

Where are they?

## WHAT'S HAPPENING HERE?

In her excitement, our new mum is not noticing or understanding the relevance of some of the things that she sees. She sees that the children are excited but does not recognise that their excitability is stress. She sees that they do not seem distressed at leaving their foster family but does not consider what this may mean in terms of forming connections. She sees that the lovely new clothes are too big, without wondering why the children are so small.

At the same time, she is literally bending over backwards to do all the 'right' things: maintaining sensory familiarity (i.e. keeping smells the same) by using the same washing powder as the foster parent, keeping the two oldest children together at night, and building familiarity with her dogs in a safe way. She really wants to nurture these children and is eager to help them feel safe and give reassurance and cuddles.

For the children the whole process is fraught, not only with terror but with the impact of the realisation for William, who is still pre-verbal, that he is a very, bad, unlovable child. It's no wonder his foster parents sent them all away; no doubt they could not wait to get rid of them. It's only a matter of time before his new mum and dad realise that.

What of the separation of the children? William is clearly showing signs of anxiety about his older sisters. He was due to see them and doesn't understand why he hasn't. It's another loss to deal with.

For Rosie, left behind in her foster family, the loss is more powerful. What does 'forever family' mean? She has been left behind with Katie. Her younger siblings are somewhere else. Somewhere she cannot imagine, with adults she doesn't know. She has always been the protector and will surely be terrified for their safety. It looks like no one thought to show Rosie and Katie where their brother and sisters were going!

## 🔆 THINK...

- ✓ Transitions are tricky for everyone. For the child:

    - What was their previous experience?

    - How will they make sense of this transition?

    - Might previous stressful memories be evoked by this new separation?

- ✓ A depth charge enters the life of the parent:

    - Who can they talk to?

    - Who will understand that this is hard for them too?

    - How can they empathise and keep the child's perspective in mind?

## 🐾 TRY THIS...

- ✓ Think about how this major transition may feel for the child:

    - Plan transitions carefully, allowing time to process.

    - Remember this process may need to be revised to suit the child's needs.

    - Be guided by the child.

    - Provide familiar objects – however old and smelly, these are vitally important for children and help them feel safe.

- ✓ Transitions are hard, and learning new ideas and new rules is hard:

    - Using visual aids and timetables can help.

- Keep activities low key.

- Be *consistent, predictable and reliable*.

✓ Look after yourself:

- Find a listening friend who will just be there for you without blaming or judging you or the child.

- Go slow – you have got a long time to get it right.

## ✎ SARAH NAISH: Thinking about reunification

I always knew that the relationship between all five children was essential and fundamental to their well-being. I could not understand how the youngest three children had been moved to us as adopters, with seemingly little regard for how this would be interpreted by Rosie and Katie.

I insisted at an early stage that Rosie and Kate were to meet with us and have some reassurance that their younger siblings were safe. This was also essential to enable us to lower Sophie and William's anxieties too. It took about a month after the youngest three came home, to organise this.

Once we had met Rosie and Katie (on Katie's 5th birthday at a family centre), I felt increasingly uncomfortable with the fact that the children had been separated, but I did not feel able to manage all five.

I knew that Rosie and Katie were with a family-finding team and there was activity searching for adopters. The girls were then 5 and 7 years.

Six months later, we all met again at a family farm. Peter and I began to feel even more uneasy about the fact that the children lived separately. We asked for Rosie and Katie to come to visit William, Sophie and Charley in our home. Once in the home environment, the deep bond between the children was striking. I was aware that family-finding had not been successful.

Peter was keen to reunite all the children. I was less sure about coping with all of them but felt it was the right thing for the children. There was some resistance from Social Services, but there were limited options.

Although there was a year between William, Sophie and Charley moving in, and then Rosie and Katie, the experiences were no less challenging. The perceived wisdom in social work is to place children in new families in birth order, but the youngest three were already well established with Peter and me before Rosie and Katie joined us.

# 5

# Honeymoon

Sarah and Peter are lucky (unlucky?) enough to experience two 'honeymoon periods', as you will read below. Honeymoon periods are a common experience for families when children first join the family. It is a time where sometimes the children may appear overly compliant. This might lull parents into a false sense of security.

These experiences vary greatly as you will see.

## ✎ SARAH NAISH: When the youngest three moved in

### Week 1

Why did I worry? My children have been at home for a week now. I really feel I am settling into my new role. Of course, it is a bit tiring, and there is not much time for me, but really things are going so well! The children eat everything I put in front of them – they have great appetites!

Charley is a typical messy baby – I just love her antics! And Sophie is so good, and she smiles and does what she is asked, with no fuss at all. She really loves her new bedroom. I think it must be lovely to have such a nice room with lovely things, and to feel how much we care for her! She seems a bit shy of coming to get a cuddle, but she always lets me hug and kiss her. The other two keep me so busy – it's just as well she is not too demanding! When little things happen and she gets cross, or if William throws his toys or rocks and sucks his thumb sometimes, I talk to my friends. It is so reassuring when they say that all children do that! Really, I don't know what I was so worried about.

**Week 3**

The children have been here three weeks and it's EXHAUSTING! The social worker warned us that the children would likely be extra clingy and need reassurance, but so far the opposite is true of Sophie. She doesn't seem to be at all clingy. Her favourite phrase is 'Me do it'. Bless! She's so independent.

William certainly needs more reassurance but seems to respond when I give it. Charley has been the most affected, I think. I know that 7 months is a bad time to move a baby. I did say this, but no one seemed to listen. I wanted to try to move the children earlier than they did.

Although it's hard work and the washing machine is literally never off (they are all in nappies), I am really enjoying it. William has continued to say 'Mummy' and that is thrilling to hear.

I feel like we are all bonding together really well and Pete seems to be taking it all in his stride and having fun with the children.

They are sleeping well so we still have our evenings, which is great.

## SARAH NAISH: When Rosie and Katie moved in – one year later

Thinking back to 'the honeymoon period' we had with the youngest three, it's interesting to see the differences with older children. Rosie is much less dependent on me and wants to parent the younger children. Luckily, they are pretty well established, so I am trying to give Rosie her childhood back. She is very helpful and seems to have similar interests to me, which is lovely. She enjoys helping me and I have seen no sign of this defiant, rude child which the foster parent described.

Katie asks everyone if they will be her new mum! When she asked me that during introductions I thought I was special. Katie does smile at me ALL the time and I definitely think she is a bit anxious. She also keeps picking up the dogs and carrying them about, but I think she just needs lots of cuddles.

## I'M OK (Katie, 6 years)

I am feeling unsafe and insecure but I'm OK. I will take care not to show you how horrible I really am. You won't want me any more when you know!

If I pretend to like all the same things as you, you will like me more and stop giving all your time to the others.

*I'm OK. I can manage on my own.*
*I don't understand the meaning of home.*
*I smile very nicely and tell you I'm fine.*
*I'm also really good at towing the line.*

*My smile is my mask to keep you away.*
*I cringe at your voice when you call out my name,*
*I can't bear your hugs or the stroke of your hand.*
*I don't trust your motives or what you have planned.*

*I stay in the background, out of the way.*
*When you ask how I'm feeling,*
*I'll say 'I'm OK.'*
*I won't ask for help or tell you I'm sad.*
*You might make me leave or think that I'm bad.*

*You don't really know me though I've been here a while.*
*I don't know myself but I know how to smile.*
*My smile is all crooked and my eyes look dead.*
*The world feels scary so I hide in my head.*

*I won't ever cry or let out my pain,*
*There'll be too much to lose and nothing to gain.*
*I'll sit in the corner, out of the way,*
*And watch all the others, learning to play.*

*Charley is noisy and makes lots of mess.*
*New Mummy just laughs at the food on her dress.*
*William is rocking and sucking his thumb,*
*I pretend to be happy but inside I feel numb.*

*I'm not that important, so I keep to myself.*
*My room's very tidy with toys on the shelf,*
*With clothes folded neatly and shoes in a row.*

*My boots are quite tight, but I won't let you know.*

*The dad says he's worried when he opens my door.*
*'You've been up here for ages and it's well after four!*
*Come down for some food and we'll go for a walk.'*
*He thinks it might help if we have a 'nice talk'.*

*I want to believe him, I want to feel safe.*
*He says he won't rush me and will move at my pace.*
*He knows that I'm worried and struggle to trust.*
*I like to keep quiet, not cause any fuss.*

*There's something about him that makes me feel sad.*
*Perhaps it's because I would like a dad.*
*I just don't feel worthy of being your child.*
*I'm damaged, unsafe and should be reviled.*

## WHAT'S HAPPENING HERE? ▀▀▀▀▀▀▀

To the parents the youngest children seemed to be adapting really well (a honeymoon period); but then, as is often the case, in reality that's not what is under the surface A year later, the parents have learned a lot and are not so easily fooled.

Loving experiences are unnatural, unsafe, uncomfortable for the children. This is terrible for them as they feel a sense of chaos, failure, shame and a world spiralling out of control. The parents may be oblivious to this conflict.

It is all about the child. Unable to trust adults, Katie shows how she is clinging on to ways to convince them that she is good, and she has learned that a quick smile, and 'I'm OK thank you, Mummy' are all that are needed to keep the tricky feelings and questions away.

Fortunately, being busy with all the other children, Mum is not looking too hard, although even that feels lonely. The child's viewpoint above could have been written by Rosie. Sophie or Katie. They feel quite invisible but also do not want to be noticed. Being noticed can be a bad thing. As far as they are concerned, none of it is 'real'.

...Even their adoptive dad, Peter. Peter seems to know that Katie feels scared, but she can't tell him how worthless she is, because if he sees the 'real' child, he might just walk out.

## ☀ THINK...

✓ Children need you to be curious about their feelings so that they can express themselves. It is OK to get it wrong, but a simple comment like 'I think I would have found it very tricky if I had moved families when I was little. I wonder if you feel a bit wobbly sometimes' lets the child know you are prepared to talk and you are trying to understand, even if you get no response or an 'I'm OK'.

# 6

# Change

Any changes in routine, whether big or small, can create chaos!

Although the family is approaching some big changes in this chapter, due to Rosie and Katie joining them, the day-to-day challenges which keep on cropping up are proving to be puzzling.

We will see how transitions, whether big or small, can be a trigger at the root of many problems.

## ✎ SARAH NAISH: Reuniting the children

As it became clearer that it would not be easy to find a family for Rosie and Katie, we became more committed to reuniting the children. This was never going to be easy. We started a big period of change. We had to move to a new house. This was no mean feat to complete with three children under the age of 5 years and carrying out introductions on a daily basis with the older two. We had to start new legal proceedings, update our assessment and return to the matching Panel. I thought we were all taking it in our stride but the youngest three became more unsettled with each passing day as reunification approached.

### A few days before reunification

It is just a few days until Rosie and Katie move in and we've all been so busy with introductions (although I think the youngest three have enjoyed seeing so much of their older sisters).

We were going to have a nice photo done and popped into the hairdresser's first. All was going quite well, and I was getting lots of compliments about how beautiful the children are, how well behaved, and so on.

Suddenly, Sophie just sat on the floor and wouldn't move! I have no idea where that came from! When I tried to pick her up, she started screaming at the top of her lungs, like I was murdering her. Honestly, it was SO embarrassing. She then lay down on the floor face down and was screaming 'NO!' As she doesn't have much language, it was hard trying to work out what she was scared of. I wondered if it was the scissors but the foster parent said she had taken them to have their hair cut a few times, so it was strange.

The hairdresser was very good about it, but I could see she had never seen quite such a spectacular tantrum before. To be honest, I'm not sure I had, and that's saying something.

I tried all the things I have used before. Talking to her, bribing her with sweets, being a bit cross, but NOTHING worked! Eventually she calmed down, but I just had to sit it out. William looked all scared and worried and Charley was getting really tetchy too.

Finally, we ran out of time and she couldn't get her hair done. Sophie seemed almost pleased!

We set off to the photographer's studio, but then she just started again. Held on to a lamppost and refused to budge. I think this was all about trying to control me. I felt like a right idiot. In the end I just picked her up and marched off. But she was screaming blue murder and it didn't feel like it was the right thing to do. I honestly think she would have stayed there all night.

We went to the photographer's and she seemed fine by then. Smiling away like nothing happened. Really strange. I hope this isn't going to be a regular thing. She is normally great, so maybe it's just delayed terrible twos?

## I'M NOT MOVING! (Sophie, 3 years)

*I didn't want to leave the park, I was having so much fun.*
*Why did she disturb me? It made me want to run.*
*Now we're at the hairdresser's, everything is loud.*
*There are far too many people, I hate being in a crowd.*
*The sounds – there are too many – rushing through my brain,*
*Then there's Mummy's voice again, driving me insane!*

*I won't get my hair cut, my hair belongs to me.*
*I'm scared that it will hurt. I'm feeling very wobbly.*
*I don't want to move from here, so I sit down on the floor.*
*I begin to scream and cry, and then I scream some more.*
*Mummy tries to move me, but I refuse to budge.*
*Her face has gone all blotchy, she offers me some fudge.*

*Go away and leave me be, I don't want to move.*
*Everything is scary, I'm not being rude.*
*I'm feeling whooshy whooshes now; I don't know what comes*
    *next.*
*I really do not care at all if my hair remains a mess.*

*Suddenly she picks me up, she says she's had enough.*
*We're all outside the door now; I think I might throw up.*
*I don't know where we're going; I just don't want to move.*
*I'm not sure what I want, but I know I want it soon.*

*I really cannot calm down, my body feels on fire.*
*Mummy says I'm safe now. I think she's a liar.*
*I cannot cope with moving from one place to another,*
*From park to shop, house to house, from mother to new*
*mother.*

## WHAT'S HAPPENING HERE?

For Mum, this was a perfectly ordinary everyday thing to do. Since they were all going to have a photograph taken, they would quickly go to have their hair done first, so that everyone would look lovely.

The children, however, may have been taken away from their favourite activities at home – even if their favourite activities are fighting and jostling for attention from Mum, these activities are familiar and safe. To be taken to a place where they receive admiration and praise is very tricky for children with extremely poor self-image.

This promotes a reaction designed to get Mum's attention back: sitting on the floor and refusing to move. Then we have to switch again and leave the hairdresser's! The whole thing is too much.

On top of these small transitions, there are very big ones happening in the background. The introductions with Katie and Rosie will be taking Mum and Dad's attention away.

What will happen when Rosie and Katie move in?

Will Sophie still have enough to eat?

These fears remain unexpressed, so seep out around other, smaller transitions. Any change is scary now.

Meanwhile, Mum is at a loss. Nothing seems to work. She has used her strategies – sitting it out did work, even if she did run out of time for a haircut, but the second incident of clinging to a lamppost on the way to the photographer's studio ended up with her forcing the issue and marching off with a screaming child – and somehow she knows this is not right. The embarrassment is only matched by her confusion about what just happened.

Change is very hard for children who have experienced trauma, because of the massive impact that changes have made on their lives. Going out, haircuts, photos – will this mean another round of meeting yet more new parents, another forever home? Being interrupted from a moment of safe play and dragged back into the real world to go somewhere that is perhaps unfamiliar – that is hard!

For many children, those rare times of escape through play are so very precious. Children who have suffered neglect and abuse have not had their survival needs met, let alone had the pleasure of playtime.

At the same time, parents may be changing too. Their ideas of how having a family would look and feel – those rosy images, those dreams for the future – all seem to be disintegrating into a chaotic mess.

## ☼ THINK...

- ✓ Changes are tricky, so plan them well and be aware of what is going on for the child.

- ✓ Try to think about times when you have had a difficult situation.

- ✓ What could you do differently?

- ✓ Are there ways to help children move on?

## ꝗ TRY THIS...

- ✓ Try to be realistic – do not plan too much in any one day.

- ✓ Leave rest time for children and adults to process the day's events.

- ✓ Base plans on your growing awareness of the limitations of your own child or children.

# 7

# Christmas

Celebration days are difficult for children who have suffered trauma, and sometimes there may be unrealistic expectations on both sides.

For the first Christmas with William, Sophie and Charley, the experience seems different to how Mum thought it would be. Before the next Christmas, Rosie and Katie have joined the family, and with that change come a whole new range of challenges!

## ✎ SARAH NAISH: Christmas with William, Sophie and Charley

The youngest three children moved in in November, so they had only been with us for four weeks before it was Christmas.

I was excited about developing lots of new family traditions. I bought Sophie the cutest little red coat. It was just so exciting being a mum, finally, at Christmas. I had waited years to experience this and I was determined to make the best Christmas I could for the children, to help to make up for some of the very miserable Christmases they had endured previously.

My friend came and helped me to decorate the Christmas tree with the children while Peter stayed in the kitchen doing some cooking. The children seemed to enjoy it but I couldn't help but notice that William looked very anxious and scared a lot of the time. When I spoke about Father Christmas he seemed even more fearful so I quickly stopped talking about that.

On Christmas Day the children were in their beds and didn't seem to want to get up. I encouraged them to come downstairs and they peeped around the lounge door with some trepidation. For some reason this made me feel so sad.

One of the presents that William opened was a doll which laughed when he squeezed the hand. As soon as it made the noise, he threw the doll across the room and ran away screaming. At the time I found it was funny but afterwards I thought how scared he must've been and I worried about the kinds of presents I might need to be careful about in the future.

Otherwise the day went quite well. The children ate dinner fine and there were no big incidents or worries. I had read about a lot of other adopters and foster parents having a horrible day. I think we were very lucky and the children seemed quite settled although more anxious than normal. I did try to keep us in the same routine and I think this helped quite a lot.

## ✎ SARAH NAISH: The second Christmas with all the children

After Rosie and Katie moved in with us, the next Christmas was very different. The girls were obsessed with looking at Argos catalogues and putting rings around the presents that they decided they wanted to have. Many letters were written with lots of lists of presents they expected. Anxiety started setting in by the end of October. When school began to change routines and bring in school play rehearsals, etc., the girls didn't cope at all. They seem to be always on edge and always scared that they were going to miss out. It didn't help that school decided to put up a 'nice list' and a 'naughty list'!! I don't know what they are thinking of sometimes!

This impacted on the youngest three children, who also then started to worry about things like Father Christmas coming into the house, and whether or not they had been good enough to get anything for Christmas among other things. Their behaviours in general just deteriorated overall.

Now I find myself beginning to dread Christmas and this is becoming worse year on year. Although I outlawed the Argos catalogues, the needs of the children and their anxieties are so overwhelming that I find I have to keep downscaling Christmas. Going to visit relatives is completely out of the equation. I also have to double-think all the presents.

It's so wearing and nothing like how I imagined it would be.

## SCARY CHRISTMAS (William, 4 years)

I'm very worried about Christmas. All the children at school are excited. I'm not sure if I am.

Mummy is very busy and Rosie has spent ages writing out silly lists from big books. I think they're called catalogues. I don't look in them though, as they are full of things I don't deserve. The teacher has a list of all the good children and another for the naughty ones. I'm trying very, very hard to stay on the good list. I can't bear to think about what might happen if I'm on the naughty list! Charley won't shut up and she's getting on my nerves. I don't know where Sophie is. Maybe she has left. Katie is in the kitchen with Mummy. She's always in the kitchen with Mummy.

Everyone is very busy and I'm not sure what we will be doing next. We went shopping earlier and the music was very loud in all the shops. After a very short time Mummy decided to take us home.

Granny came round with a lovely cake. Rosie and Katie haven't stopped talking about it. They are being very nice to Granny.

I'm not sure if I will be getting any presents this year. Bad children don't deserve nice things.

I remember last year when Mummy gave me a very colourful parcel. I felt a bit wobbly when I opened it but I tried to keep smiling. Inside was a very scary doll. It laughed when I squeezed its hand. I thought it was real and threw it across the room. I've never forgotten that doll. Sometimes I dream about it coming alive at night. I hope I don't get another one this year!

The teacher keeps talking about Father Christmas. He looks very, very scary. I don't want a strange man coming into our house. What if he 'gets' me; what if he takes me away. Where will I go?

My eyes are all watery and I look at the table, hoping that Mummy won't notice. She does.

My tummy and my head are hurting and I'm feeling wobbly, very, very wobbly.

## WHAT'S HAPPENING HERE?

The adult expectations simply do not equate with the children's reality. William shows us clearly that his internal working model (see Appendix 1) is in direct conflict with Christmas mythology – he knows he is naughty. He is very bad. He does not deserve to have things which are intended for 'nice children'.

Judging by the reaction of the young ones in the first Christmas scenario, none of them knew what to expect. Fortunately, Mum realises that things are not right and that they seem to be scared. She instinctively reduces the excitement levels and keeps to familiar routines to help the little ones cope.

# ⋅ॣ⋅ THINK...

✓ What is there to be afraid of? It's Christmas! But for William, who has suffered from severe neglect and abuse, reality is a very different thing:

- Big men coming down the chimney, laughing, to 'get them'? Terrifying.

- 'Elf on the shelf', watching their every move? Who sent it? What is it telling? To whom? Maybe it will magically tell tales to the birth family, and then they will come and get the children.

- Even the gifts are worrying – a doll that looks scary (it may have triggered old memories), laughs when you touch it – has it come to life? What will happen?

- Maybe gifts have been given, only to be taken away or destroyed.

## Disintegration of routine

Our children need consistency, predictability and reliability to help them to build new neurological pathways (as described in Room 1, Introduction). It's hard enough to do this within a structure, but when the structure fails and things become chaotic and unexpected, anxiety becomes very heightened. It feels like everything is changing. Does that mean the adults will change too, and become as scary as the adults in the children's past were?

## Sensory overwhelm and stress

Many of our children find it hard to manage very 'busy' situations where there is lots of excitement. Hence the scenario where they always 'ruin' lovely days out – they simply cannot deal with crowds, excitement, noise and bustle – the additional stress very quickly sends them into overwhelm (the feeling of being unable to process any more information, sensations or emotions, which often leads to a fight/flight response), and they do not have the resources to self-regulate or rationalise their experience and reframe it as positive.

Christmas is intense on a sensory level. Lights, bells, songs, presents, decorations, colour, veiled threats ('naughty' and 'nice' lists) all combine to make it impossible to manage.

## Less is more

We live in a society where all too often we equate lots of 'things' as being necessary to express affection, love and caring. Our children need support to be able to accept such unconditional gestures of love; and so when Mum has a limit on gifts, and organises a carefully thought-out, pared-down occasion, this is a way to help William, Rosie, Katie, Sophie and Charley to manage by ensuring that they are not overwhelmed.

Sarah Naish has written a book, *The Very Wobbly Christmas*, which can be a very useful tool to use with children as Christmas approaches. It helps children to express their worries and enables them to see that these anxieties are recognised by the parent.

# 8

# The Honeymoon
# Is Over

Many parents find that after an initial period where the children have been compliant or wary, there is a distinct change. This is hardly ever for the better and can be a challenging time.

Things are beginning to get tricky, as Sarah struggles with the relentless nature of parenting. Parenting is relentless. Her children do not respond to any of her skills from her professional life. They just do not seem to be like other children she has experienced, and she is having to look at new strategies to help her children, rather than the children adapting to a new way of life! For the children, the struggles continue, as we will see.

✎ SARAH NAISH: William, Sophie and Charley
– six weeks after they came home

I think we can safely say the honeymoon is over. It's not dreadful, but I am definitely feeling an air of relentless drudgery! Sophie is struggling to settle at night and I am up and down the stairs most nights. Her tantrums have continued and I am having to learn new strategies fast!

William is making progress but seems so fearful of everything. I was hoping we would make some progress with potty training but I think it will be a miracle if we get anywhere in the next six months. With all of them in nappies it's hard going.

Sophie and William are due to start nursery, but the initial visit didn't go well with them both screaming and clinging on to me. They are also terrified of flies, the beach and the sea. Tricky as we live on the sea front!

Charley is quite delayed but pretty easy to care for. She doesn't seem to like me very much though and clearly favours Peter. This makes me sad as she is the only baby I will ever have and I had really hoped she would be more deeply connected to me.

Peter seems to be very focused on Charley and is leaving the older ones to me, which is causing us some strain.

## SARAH NAISH: Rosie (8 years) and Katie (6 years) – eight weeks after they came home

When I met Katie during the introductions, she asked me if I would be her new mummy. I was so happy about this, but now I have heard her asking about six different women so it's not quite as meaningful! She follows me around everywhere and smiles all the time. I can't get her to express any opinion or make any choices and she always defers to Rosie, who is 'boss'.

Rosie was very compliant and helpful for the first eight weeks, but over the last week I have seen her become more and more controlling. She has refused to call me 'Mum', preferring instead to use my first name.

I'm not pushing this as I don't know what the word 'Mum' means to her. The only way I can describe her at present is 'brooding'. She glowers all the time at everyone and will try to get in sneaky punches and pinches to the younger ones if I am not 100% vigilant.

## THE REAL ME (Rosie, 8 years)

I've tried very hard to hold all my big wobbly feelings inside but they just won't stay in anymore.

Since we moved back in with our brother and sisters, I've been doing my best to make sure the adults like me the most. If they like me, they might not hurt me.

I bet it's only a matter of time though before we have to leave, or worse...

I keep my angry face on to make the adults stay away.

Katie is always in the way. She follows the mummy everywhere and is always asking for food all day long. What if there isn't enough for me? I don't want that growling feeling in my tummy again. I don't want to be locked in the scary room.

I hit out at them all, I shout at them if they get too near. Sophie is still keeping everyone awake at night and I think the mummy and daddy will soon get angry and I'll be the one who gets hurt.

I'd better show them that I can and will protect myself. I don't need them. I don't need anyone.

The mummy says I look sad. What has she seen? I look away, I won't cry.

I like it when I make them cross. It makes me feel in charge. I have decided that I won't listen to the adults. I always says 'no' whenever they ask me to do something.

I don't know what's going to happen next, so I need to make sure I am in control. I feel very scared but I won't ever let them see that.

My brother is chewing all his clothes again. He is always making those weird wailing noises at night and keeping everyone up. The mummy said he had stopped doing that before we moved in. My fault then!

Charley is constantly making stupid noises and the daddy won't put her down. She throws everything on the floor and the noise hurts my ears. I pinch her when no one is looking.

Her screams sound vaguely familiar – screams from the scary place, the cold place, the wet place, the dark place.

## WHAT'S HAPPENING HERE?

Here we see Sarah waking up to the realities facing her in her individual circumstances. The children do not seem to be settling, Peter is only responsive to one of the children, and this feels unhelpful and unsupportive (we'll find out more about Dad's perception in Chapter 18, 'Exhaustion (Compassion Fatigue)'. The children do not seem to be coping or making progress like other children Sarah knows. She is really stepping up her game, and realising that she needs to find new strategies to deal with the emerging behaviours, but this is so tiring, and we can sense that there is some feeling of isolation creeping in.

Meanwhile, Rosie in particular is showing us her thoughts and they are very revealing – the lack of early childhood attunement (the reflected connection between parent and child) and stimulus, and also her other experiences, mean that she has no sense of 'her' mummy or daddy. They are 'the' mummy and daddy. They are easily interchangeable with other mummies and daddies.

The most likely thing is they will show their true colours soon, and she has no trust. Best to stay in control of them and the environment. 'The' mummy seems to have noticed she is sad inside. That feels scary. Better lock her out quick. If you let mummies and daddies get too close, they blame you, hurt you, forget to feed you, and send you away.

## ⚙ THINK...

✓ The children in this family are lucky. Their mum is realising that, for the children to change, she has to change her parenting style. She knows that they behave the way they do as a result of their earliest experiences and that this has affected their internal working model of themselves, and mummies and daddies and the world.

- Do you need to change your own ideas?

- What experiences have your children had?

- How will this affect the way they expect mummies and daddies or adults to behave?

- What will their experiences have led them to believe about themselves?

- What do you think their internal working model will be?

✓ When a child has missed out on so many developmental tasks that happen in an attuned relationship, they find things much more difficult to learn. If they have been very unsafe, they will find things even harder. One of these developmental tasks is object permanency – children typically develop this at around 8 months old when they start looking for objects that disappear from view, including their parents. Separation from the object usually results in separation anxiety and we expect this to last a few months.

✓ The child with no sense of parent (as we would understand the word), and who has been ignored and neglected, can perceive any adult as being appropriate to get their needs met. There is no sense of a parent who is there for you specifically. A child who knows that adult help is required to ensure their needs are met might approach any adult – safe or not. They will certainly not rely on Mum or Dad, and would rather learn to manage by themselves. The child is the only constant in their own life.

# 9

# Emotional Age

One of the hardest things for parents, professionals, teachers and connected others to grasp is that our children's physical development and the number of years they have achieved so far are not always an accurate indicator of where they are developmentally.

Even though the youngest three have been home for just over a year, with Rosie and Katie a more recent addition, the parents are struggling with reconciling the functioning ages with the children's chronological ones.

✎ SARAH NAISH: How old are you?

William is just 4 years old, and only recently started school. Sophie is 3 years old and at nursery. Charley is still home with me as she is 18 months old.

It's very confusing though, as my children never seem to be behaving at the age they really are. It makes it impossible with school as they are always saying things like, 'He has to learn', or 'At 4 we expect...'

My instinct is that the children are really much younger. If they received no stimulation or input for the first one to four years of their lives, how can they now be at the same point 'in the race' as the child who *did* have their needs met and were responded to?

Katie is 6 years old but is having play therapy and the therapist insists she has a baby bottle. I find this really difficult as she walks round with it permanently attached to her mouth. My old 'nursery nursing' strategies want to take the bottle off her and tell her she needs to be 'a big girl', but my instinct says she needs to experience this stage. I can't imagine she had many nurturing feeding times as a baby, so even though I do find it very hard I am feeding her on my lap like a baby and trying to put back in some of the early lost nurture.

Sophie and William are both very small and developmentally about two years behind, so in a way that is lucky as everyone, including me, treats them as younger children.

Rosie seems very mature for her age. She is only 8 years old but she is so street-wise. She is overly independent and still insists on calling me by my first name, not 'Mum'. She likes to do everything for herself. I think she is a very frightened little girl who cannot trust adults. I am working hard to try to help her to relax a bit more into her childhood and let go of the reins. This is proving very difficult.

I often feel that I have one 14-year-old in the house and then 1-year-old quads! I wonder how long this will last.

Will they EVER catch up? It is a worry. Social workers talk about 'global developmental delay', where apparently everything is running a few months or years behind, but I think – I hope – it's just 'playing catch-up'...


## ❦ BADLY BEHAVED? (Any child)

*What I do*
*And what they say...*

*I like to throw things around.*
*'I hope you pick them up afterwards.'*

*I can't calm myself down.*
'Why?'

*I have big issues with food.*
'Oh, that's annoying.'

*I have wee and poo issues and sometimes I smear.*
'Ugh, that's disgusting.'

*I make a big mess everywhere.*
'How unfair on everyone else.'

*I often hit out at people.*
'You'll soon stop when they hit you back.'

*I struggle to make friends.*
'I'm not surprised.'

*I can be cruel to animals.*
'You should be ashamed of yourself.'

*I am frightened to do what you say.*
'Just start listening and doing as you're told.'

*I sometimes run away.*
'How can you put others through that worry?'

*I often use a whiny voice.*
'Oh, grow up.'

*I can't express my emotions very well.*
'That's just an excuse for bad behaviour.'

*Sometimes I say things I shouldn't.*
'Learn to zip it then.'

*I am rude to adults.*
'You should learn some manners.'

*I make a mess of my clothes.*
*'You need to learn to look after things.'*

*I make an even bigger mess of my room.*
*'Well, blinking tidy it up then.'*

*I often tell tall stories.*
*'You mean you're a liar.'*

*I took sweets from the shop without paying.*
*'Thief.'*

*I often forget to say 'please' and 'thank you'.*
*'How ungrateful.'*

*I struggle to fall asleep and often keep others awake.*
*'Selfish.'*

*I talk a lot and ask lots of silly questions.*
*'Oh, give it a break.'*

*I follow my parents around everywhere.*
*'You need to give others their own space.'*

*I often cry and scream when I want something.*
*'HOW OLD ARE YOU?'*

*I'm a toddler.*

## WHAT'S HAPPENING HERE?

Mum is aware that the children are behaving much younger than they actually are. While the social workers are talking about scary things such as 'global developmental delay' (which certainly can be an issue with children who have suffered severe neurological damage), her instinct is that what they need is time to experience the developmental stages which they missed out on – and she is quite right about this.

Neurological damage is damage which has occurred either in utero (for example due to alcohol or misuse of drugs) or to damage sustained after birth (such as shaking a baby and causing literal physical damage or oxygen starvation during a difficult birth). Neural damage can affect development in all areas including physical development causing different levels of physical or learning disability.

Our ideas and understanding of ourselves and the world around us are built from our experiences as we mature, explore and learn under the guidance of a safe, secure and attuned adult.

Developmental delay is the result of a failure of an early attuned relationship – so the priorities of the growing child change from the child who has a secure adult base and who engages in exploration and learning to the child who has suffered neglect and/or abuse and is focused on survival.

The child's voice in the poem above (which could be applied to any of the children in this book) talks about the judgement and lack of understanding they suffer because of the way that they are trying to engage with their learning and development stages. So a child of 11 may have areas of development which are much younger and still need to play the same games or be drawn to toys which would be associated with a much younger age group, or they may need help because they do not have age appropriate social skills.

None of the behaviours listed are unusual or unheard of, but they typically belong to a much younger child (1–2 years old). Where emerging communication gives rise to nonsense chatter, there is a need to keep parents close (or they just disappear). All sensory data is interesting and to be explored (including poo and wee), and strong feelings of frustration and disappointment are unmanageable, leading to screaming, tantrums, kicking, and lashing out.

This child needs to be supported as if they were a toddler, to enable them to learn to give names to their strong feelings, to learn that an adult will help them, and (big, big issue) to learn that *some* adults *can* be trusted.

This is much harder for the child who has reached an age beyond the developmental window (the optimal time for specific learning to take place) for this to occur; but to help change their internal working model and rewire the brain, it has to happen.

When children are stressed, they regress. Their 'thinking brain' may also be 'offline'. This makes it difficult to make and store new memories and to retain a sense of predictability. Our children, therefore, live in the NOW...like toddlers do.

Our ideas and understanding of ourselves and the world around us are built from our experiences as we mature, explore and learn under the guidance of a safe, secure and attuned adult.

## Different areas of development

Development does not simply happen as we get older – it is forged and nurtured within our relationships and communities. Physically, a child is likely to grow and develop their physical body. If I child has been neglected, they may be very small, but are likely to catch up later. They will enter puberty and go through the usual changes as these are biologically determined. Other areas of development, however, are mediated through experiences and relationships, including:

- physical ability

- emotional development – understanding your own and others' feelings

- social development – understanding social rules, norms, and manners

- cognitive development – the ability to learn, process and recall.

It is entirely possible for a child to be functioning at different levels with these developmental stages.

We've included a section at the back of this book to help you to understand typical developmental stages (see Appendix 2).

## 💡 THINK...

- ✓ Spend some time observing your child: their actions, their conversations, their emotional responses.

- ✓ Think about the emotional age your child is acting, not their actual age.

- ✓ How would you usually treat a child with their emotional age?

## 🔖 TRY THIS...

- ✓ It is hard to parent in a developmental-appropriate rather than an age-appropriate way, but try parenting your child with their emotional age in mind. For example, think 'toddler'. Is your child able to link cause and effect yet?

- ✓ Remember self-care, and find people you trust to support you, especially in school and friendship groups.

# 10

# When Things Get Stuck

Like many parents who are parenting children who have suffered trauma, Sarah is struggling with trying to understand WHY her children do the things they do. Behaviours seem to come out of nowhere and, on top of that, the children are unable to link cause and effect. This feels like Groundhog Day!

## ✎ SARAH NAISH: One step forwards, two steps back

I do feel like we are living in Groundhog Day! I have to repeat myself so often and every time it's either like new information or the children simply do not care. It doesn't matter how many times I explain that if you leave the bath taps on, the bath will flood, or if they go out without a coat on they will get cold. They seem totally unable to imagine or care about what happens next. This means that I already know to throw away my reward charts. I've also stopped bothering with, 'If you don't..., x will happen.' It's pointless.

More puzzling, (and worrying) is that when we go back-wards it seems to come out of nowhere. Today we were all sitting in the kitchen playing with some play-doh and suddenly

William started screaming and crying and running out the back door. All the children looked puzzled and I had no idea what was going on. I followed him outside and hugged him to try to help him calm down. He wasn't making any sense – just crying and screaming and pointing. I couldn't get him to come back in the kitchen for over half an hour. After a couple of hours I managed to work out that he was scared of a fly that had come into the room. It's really hard to know when this kind of thing might happen.

I had the same reactions last week when we went down to the beach. This was the first time the children had seen the sea, and suddenly Sophie and William were literally climbing up me screaming hysterically. I'm sure people around us thought that something terrifying had just happened, but from the look on their faces something actually had.

Last week the school phoned me to say that Sophie was crying and could not be consoled. When I went up there, she was still sitting outside the Headmistress's room and no one could comfort her. I ended up taking her home.

I tried everything...guessing, telling her what I thought it was, etc., but nothing seemed even close. Sometimes I just don't seem able to reach the children. They seem like they're in a different place, and when they look at me I don't feel like they're seeing me but something else. I can never tell what triggers these episodes of terror or extreme sadness. I just know that I have to stay with them and keep trying to get them back to me.

As a parent I think it's one of the most frustrating things. Just as I start to feel like I am getting somewhere, I am suddenly looking at this child in front of me like they are crazy. It's very scary.

## ✂ I'M STUCK (Any child)

*I feel such scary wobbles that make my body shake.*
*I fall into Room 1 again, but my body doesn't break.*
*I cannot tell you where I am or how to find me there,*
*But please don't leave me in Room 1, it's more than I can bear.*
*I have big worries deep inside my brain.*
*They alert me when there's danger, over and over again.*
*I haven't got the power to switch them off on my own,*
*I need someone to help me, to know I'm not alone.*
*You say I will get cold outside but I live here and now.*
*You always warn me what to do; you're just a silly cow.*
*I don't care what happens next, I can't imagine that.*
*Nothing that I ever did changed anything in fact.*
*Often, I'm confused and get a false alarm.*
*I'm sure that I'm in danger, when really there's no harm.*
*I've got lots of scary memories stored inside of me*
*And sometimes I simply cannot tell what's the enemy.*
*The problem that I have is I can't tell truth from lies.*
*I think that all adults are monsters in disguise.*
*I often overreact to stuff that's not a risk.*
*Even if an adult's safe, I can't tell that he/she is.*
*Sometimes I will freeze or start to run away*
*Or I switch off all your words, so I don't hear what you say.*
*If only others realised I haven't got a choice,*
*When I perceive a threat, I am the loudest voice.*
*You have no way of knowing when I'll fall into Room 1.*
*My brain's offline, my terror real, my legs begin to run.*

## ✂ UNLOVED (Sophie, 4 years)

Last week Mummy had to come up to the school and get me.
We had been doing words with Mrs Bentley. Mrs Bentley was

explaining how you can put 'un' in front of a word to change it to the opposite. When she changed 'loved' to 'unloved' I felt a fally, whooshy feeling and all I could see was my brother crying, sad and lonely. I couldn't stop crying. I couldn't talk. When Mummy came, I could still see my brother. I tried to stare at Mummy more so I could stop seeing my brother. I am trying to come back.

Don't follow me into Room 1. Stay safe in Room 2.

But come and get me. Give me your hand. Help me to find my way home.

I can't do it on my own.

## WHAT'S HAPPENING HERE?

There are two different things happening which have ended up making Sarah's family all feel very stuck.

Firstly, the children are struggling to link cause and effect. This results in some very worrying and frustrating moments. In the children's early life nothing made much sense. If they were wet and cried, no one came; if they were hungry, they were met with an abusive response. So, what have they learned? They have learned that they have no impact on the world, that their needs do not matter and must be ignored, and that whatever they do it does not change anything. If a child's early life was one spent living in chaos, then there is no predictability, and hence no ability to form the patterns which enable cause and effect reasoning.

The children, therefore, are living in the NOW – they are unable to fast forward and imagine how they might feel if they go outside without a coat on, for example. This, combined with faulty neuroception (the recognition of sensations such as temperature, hunger, toilet urges), gives everyone a problem! In other words, they have no empathy for their 'future self'. They cannot imagine how they might feel later, and they do not care. Their brains are hardwired for survival in the here and now!

Secondly, in the examples above, Sophie was catapulted into 'Room 1' (see the Introduction for a reminder) at school, by the use of one word. The children also fell into Room 1 when they saw the sea and the fly. How difficult is this for us to manage as parents?

## ♟ REMEMBER...

✓ As therapeutic parents, we are always trying to work out WHERE behaviours come from. If we keep meeting the behaviour with the wrong response (because we have not worked out the true cause), then we *cannot* resolve the issue.

✓ We *must* avoid asking the child *why* they did something, at ALL costs! The children do not know why – they are merely following their body's direction.

✓ These intense responses, like the fight/flight response (see Glossary), are unconscious. The body responds to the perceived threat BEFORE we are aware of the trigger which is buried deep in our memory (like a phobia response). At this point the oldest systems in the brain take over and will activate whatever is needed to survive without thinking about it. It is not unusual for children not to remember what they did while they are in this state.

## ♞ TRY THIS...

✓ If you are trapped in a cycle of behaviours where you are repeating the same response to that behaviour, try changing your response and see what happens.

✓ One of the most powerful tools we can give our children is to 'name the need'. We must try to work out the WHY for them. Once we have worked this out or made our best guess, we tell the child. This gives them an alternative inner dialogue and explanation for their behaviours (e.g. 'I'm not bad. I got upset because X happened to me when I was little.').

✓ When a child has 'fallen into Room 1', you can use that analogy to help them understand what happened. This must be done out of the moment when their thinking brain is online.

✓ Stay close and available with a child who is 'in Room 1'. It is your calm presence which will help them to regulate (calm down) and exit.

# 11

# Food

One of the common experiences that affects parents of children with developmental trauma is the peculiar relationship that the children seem to have with food – it just does not make sense.

## ✎ SARAH NAISH: Food nightmares

It's really strange but the children seem to move between eating everything in sight or nothing being good enough!

Sophie only likes to eat 'beige food' and doesn't like it touching! So funny (not). I put it in the blender and we don't seem to have a problem now. Katie picks at her food and pretends not to want it. She thinks I don't notice but she always eats it.

I have decided that I cannot do lots of different meals and try to cater to everyone's tastes.

The children can eat and eat and never seem to be full. I can literally give them a roast dinner with pudding and they will be saying they are hungry within minutes!

Sitting at the table together is a challenge. Where are the fun family mealtimes I thought we would have? Rosie dominates the conversation and does not like me interacting with the others. This makes it very tiring and we have to manage everyone's time individually.

I have noticed that the children will often hide food away, especially the older two. Sophie likes to try to save her food for as long as possible.

Charley is great and eats everything with no fuss as all. The oldest four are reliant on high intakes of sugar. We have to be very careful what we leave lying about!

I know their diet was not healthy at all in their birth family. It was erratic and the children were underweight when they were removed. I know they did not know when they would next eat, and this has created a lot of uncertainty for them around food. I make sure we have regular mealtimes and that there are snack times too. Always at the same time. I think this is starting to help them to calm down and trust me that they are going to be able to eat!

One thing that is very annoying is that if the meal is literally one minute late they start circling me in the kitchen! I feel like I am being hunted and cannot move. I can't describe how cross this makes me but I know it's not a reasonable feeling, so I don't say anything. Just huff and sigh a bit!

## ⟐ WHAT FOOD MEANS (Rosie, 8 years)

At times I'm really scared I won't be fed. When I lived with my birth parents, we would often go without food and I'd have to go to bed with an empty tummy. During mealtimes I watch everyone's plate to make sure we all have equal portions, (unless it's something I don't like, of course).

Katie and I sneak food into our bedrooms just in case we wake up hungry during the night. Sweet stuff is even better as it helps with the scary feelings in my chest. I'm not sure if the others do it, but Katie and I have always helped each other with getting food.

## ⋐ TIME FOR DINNER

*Sitting at the table is really very scary.*
*Adults are too close, and I'm feeling very wary,*
*Watching all our movements as we shovel in the food.*
*Katie's pigging everything, but they say I'm being rude!*

*I don't like stupid carrots but I really like the pie.*
*I take a bit of Sophie's and then she starts to cry.*
*Sarah says, 'Don't do that,' but I just carry on.*
*I don't care if she's angry, I quite like feeling wrong!*

*Charley's very chatty and eats up all her veg.*
*Sarah looks like she's cracking up and verging on the edge.*
*William eats quietly, he hasn't raised his head.*
*Sophie looks quite funny when her face is very red.*

*Sarah asks her nicely if she'd like some of the pie.*
*Sophie says she's fine, but I know that is a lie.*
*Charley just keeps shovelling, she hasn't got much left.*
*She asks Sarah for her pudding but is told to 'have a rest'.*

*Sophie's even redder and looks like she might pop.*
*Sarah's getting cross now and shouts we need to stop.*
*Dinner time is over and I need to clear my plate.*
*I do it very slowly as I want to stay up late.*

*Charley's very whiny and hasn't had her drink.*
*Sarah starts complaining that she can't even think!*
*I reach into the cupboard when Sarah's in the loo,*
*I grab a load of biscuits then don't know what to do.*

*Katie comes to help me and puts them up her skirt.*
*We'd better get out of here before we get hurt.*
*We slope off to the bedroom, hide the biscuits in the drawer,*
*But Sarah's right behind us as some fall on the floor.*
*Katie screams and lies a lot, says 'It wasn't me!'*
*Oh, here we go again, let's blame Rosie Rudey!*

## ⟁ WHY FOOD MAKES ME WOBBLY

*I haven't got those pathways built to let me know*
*That you will always feed me and you'll never let me go.*
*I truly cannot recognise when my tummy is quite full,*
*Or believe that you will feed me when I get back home from*
  *school.*
*I'm not just being greedy, it's a need to stay alive.*
*Food is often hoarded as I'm wired to survive.*
*I think you might have noticed that I always clear my plate,*
*Then tell you that I'm hungry when it's getting rather late.*
*Babies should have parents who get up in the night*
*To feed them if they're crying, rock them till they're right.*
*That wasn't my experience: No one came to see,*
*No one even cared if my bed was full of wee.*

## WHAT'S HAPPENING HERE?

Poor Sarah. She is turning herself inside out to manage mealtimes, and we can see how her insights about her children's earlier lives are beginning to help her, but she has not connected all the dots yet. She has not realised that the over-dependence on cheap food and sugar can cause an addiction, but she can see that she has to be careful with sugary foods. She knows that mealtimes were scarce, so she is very careful to maintain a routine, but it will take a long time for this to take effect for the children. Unfortunately, the very presence of adults during meals feels intimidating, and she is feeling sadness about the happy shared meals she expected.

The children are so insecure about food that they show their anxiety by 'circling in the kitchen' if there is a delay. Rosie does not realise she can request more food – she steals it quickly while no one is looking. Even her siblings are rivals for her survival – if they get too much food, there will not be enough for her.

In addition, on the rare occasions Sophie got food, it was always cheap, processed 'beige' food. No fresh fruit or vegetables. These colourful tasty additions to their diet seem very strange.

Even though they have just eaten, Rosie and Katie have to steal biscuits so that there is food available (because who knows when this mum will show her true colours and stop feeding them) and also to fuel sugar cravings. The other children show individual food stress responses: shovel it in quick (before it gets taken away); make it last (helps you feel full); keep quiet and avoid being noticed; chat and distract. These responses are based on previous experiences that have shaped their whole attitude to mealtimes, parents and food.

As the family begins to adjust, some of the most challenging issues remain unresolved. (In Chapter 12, 'Sugar', there is a whole section dealing with sugar addiction.)

To start to unpick this, we need to be thinking about the experience of the child. There are three things to think about:

## Hungry for love

The child who was ignored, not picked up, not calmed down, not reassured by an adult; but who was always handed a bottle, a biscuit or a sweet to 'shut them up', will learn to look to food for comfort. Any emotional wobble or worry will see them looking for food to fill the empty feeling inside. These children do not trust adults, they trust food.

## Cruelty and neglect

The child who has been starved, had food withheld as a punishment, or been inappropriately and irregularly fed, will be fixated on this survival need. They will eat everything, steal food, be indiscriminate about their food and really panic if there is no food available when they need it. Not having food has literally presented a survival stress for them.

**Rejecting nurture**

The children accept nurture alongside accepting food. Therefore, if they want to reject your nurturing, as Rosie longs to here, they may reject your food.

## ☀ THINK...

✓ Think about your own child's behaviour around food – do any of the three things above sound familiar?

## ☀ TRY THIS...

✓ Create a pictorial timetable of meals and snacks showing what food will be available at these times. The child can be reminded to check this.

✓ Check out *The A–Z of Therapeutic Parenting* by Sarah Naish, which has more strategies on managing mealtimes.

# 12

# Sugar

Children who have suffered trauma often seem to need very high levels of sugar intake, which can cause problems in a number of ways.

As time goes on in Sarah Naish's family, more problems surface. As well as the problems with food in general, sugar is a causing a lot of difficulties in the home.

## ✎ SARAH NAISH: Sick

Sometimes the amount of sugar that Rosie can eat makes me feel physically sick! All the children seem to be on a mission to cram themselves as full as possible with biscuits, sweets and cakes.

Throughout the day I do make sure that they have snacks to help with their addiction – it really is an addiction. I've tried everything. I have tried getting all the sugar out of the house (not easy). I've tried telling others to stop giving them sweets, but they just do it anyway but in a more sneaky way.

It makes me so frustrated because I'm sure people think I'm a really horrible person as I am determined to stop them having so much sugar. They don't seem to realise that if I wasn't strict the children would eat sugar the whole time! I worry about their teeth and them putting on weight – they literally would have chocolate for breakfast, dinner and tea if allowed. Nothing seems to be enough and Easter will be a nightmare, I'm sure! I've tried putting lots of fruit in the fruit bowl. When we went strawberry picking, they almost ate their own bodyweight in fruit!

Rosie in particular will try to get in the cupboards and has even eaten things like the little sugar star decorations that go on top of cakes. Yesterday I found six mini roll wrappers under Katie's bed, which weren't there before. I also find wrappers which are clearly from other children's lunch boxes or 'gifts' from children at school. Last week, Katie's teacher said that stuff was going missing from other children's lunches and snacks – but, funnily enough, none of the savoury items!

We have sweets once a week on Saturday, which is quite handy because the children will literally do anything to get their sweet money, so it's a good time to tidy bedrooms!

## MUM, I'M STARVING! (Rosie, 8 years)

*What if you don't feed me and I'm starving late at night?*
*I've nicked biscuits from the cupboard, then caused an awful*
  *fight.*
*Jackie hardly fed me and my belly used to growl,*
*So when you're fast asleep, I am often on the prowl.*

*I know I've been here ages and you say you'll meet my needs*
*But I'm lonely in my room and I've never had night feeds.*
*No one ever got up and rocked me when I cried,*
*So my need remains unmet and I'm wobbly inside.*

*Underneath my bed I hide a little stash*
*Of chocolate, crisps and biscuits and a pack of instant mash.*

*I know I shouldn't do it and I'm wracked with toxic shame,*
*But the urge just overtakes me and I carry on the same.*

*I've got these dreadful feelings and a whir inside my brain.*
*I'm desperate for the sugar like an addict on cocaine.*
*The sugar helps the whirring and gives me a great high,*
*Then afterwards it's worse as my fists begin to fly.*

*I can't wait 'til the weekend when I get a bit of cash.*
*Straight down to the shops for chocolate and flapjacks.*
*I spend my pocket money on sweet stuff, crisps and drink.*
*They're gone within the hour before you can even blink.*

I am hungry. I am always hungry. Don't tell me I just ate because that was AGES ago. Well I can't actually tell the time but it FEELS like ages ago.

I am not hungry for an apple. No, actually I am only hungry for sweets. I definitely need sweets because that's the only thing that stops the tippy tappy feelings in my arms and legs.

When I feel fizzy, my legs rush about to find cake, sweets and biscuits.

I can't believe you have locked them in a cupboard. Are you actually trying to KILL me?

Well, ha ha! I know where Sophie's secret stash is and I am going to get it. She will never know it's me. I HAVE to eat them all right now so the fizzies stop.

What does 'full up' even feel like? Does that mean it's poking out of your mouth? Is that what sick is? Does that mean I have to keep eating until I'm sick so I know I'm full?

Well you just think I am a pig because I need all these cakes and sweets, so I am going to eat all that as fast as I can but I'm going in the loo to do it.

That's better. But I am sure I am still hungry...

## WHAT'S HAPPENING HERE?

Firstly, there is a *sugar addiction*. Yes, sugar is addictive. For children, the 'rush' from sugar is equivalent in addictive terms to class A drugs. Children get quickly addicted to sugar which is present in cheap, processed drinks, foods and cereals, as well as sweets.

Rosie has suffered neglect, and these are the very foods she and her siblings had access to. Children with a sugar addiction will need to have this very carefully managed, and will steal, hide and overindulge to satisfy their craving.

Secondly, there are the *unmet needs of the baby*. Rosie was denied regulation by her birth parents but instead maybe (on a good day) got a bottle or a biscuit to shut her up. A child with this experience learns three things:

1. Adults do not help you feel better.

2. Food helps you feel better.

3. Sugar helps you feel better still!

4. These children will look for food as their secure base. Food always delivers.

Of course, the emotional need is still unmet, and will remain unmet until a parent with knowledge, patience and love comes along to name the need and gradually fill the terrible hungry hole in the child's emotional self. I call this 'the hungry heart'.


## 🏆 REMEMBER...

✓ The child who steals and hoards is a fearful child, whose hardwired responses drive behaviours that ensure that food must be eaten when it is available. There is no experience of regular feeding, and building this understanding will take time. This is not naughtiness, or wilful stealing. It is survival behaviour and must be seen as such.

✓ The child will need reminding *all the time* that you are aware of their needs and will meet them.

✓ Sometimes the child may be hungry for a hug, not a snack.

## ♞ TRY THIS...

✓ Make sure a fruit bowl is always available.

✓ Buy a personal snack box that can be refilled every day.

✓ Consider having a separate snack box for school – if the child feels scared or stressed, they may need this in order not to steal.

✓ Try to offer comfort and empathy alongside the food.

✓ Visit this website for mor useful ideas: www.beating addictions.co.uk/SugarAddiction.html.

# 13

# Easter

Following on from the family's experiences with food and sugar, Easter was never going to be easy! This is a light-hearted look at one of our favourite holidays – especially as it allows lots of access to one of our much-loved treats!

✎ SARAH NAISH: The night before Easter

*'Twas the night before Easter,*
*And nothing did stir,*
*Mummy had wine.*
*It was all a nice blur.*
*The chocolate was hidden,*
*The children asleep,*
*No drama at bedtime,*
*Not even a peep*
*The huge chocolate eggs, a nice tempting prize,*
*Had sweetened the children to soon close their eyes.*

*Apart from one house.*

*The house on the corner had all its lights on,*
*The children were screaming, the Easter eggs gone!*
*The eggs had been eaten, but NO ONE had seen them,*
*(Just chocolate and handprints with sick in between them).*

*The parents asked why, but the children denied it.*
*(They knew not to say Rosie had supplied it.)*
*The youngest admitted she'd 'just had a lick',*
*The dog wandered past, hopefully eyeing the sick.*

*The parents soon tired of all the mad lying,*
*The blaming and shouting, the pointing and crying.*
*'It's just such a shame,' Mum said with sad face,*
*'As now there's no time for eggs to be replaced!'*

*Next morning at breakfast their faces were sad,*
*It looked like remorse, but Mum could not be had.*
*She'd found the egg wrappers all under their bed.*
*No Easter eggs – 'Natural consequences,' she said.*

*She shared in their sadness and nurtured their pain,*
*Then later they went for a walk in the rain.*
*When they returned, they all helped to make*
*A rather nice chocolate Easter cake!*

*(Which they then argued about.)*

## ⌘ WHY I WOBBLE AT EASTER (Katie, 6 years)

*Easter was when they first took me into care.*
*I didn't know who I'd stay with and I didn't know where.*
*I was only 4 years old so I can't really remember.*
*But it was certainly March or April, definitely not September.*
*The lady gave us chocolate, a tiny little rabbit.*
*Chocolate made me happy, so I soon developed a habit.*
*Sugar rushing through me, melting all the fear.*
*She tried to hug my sister, but I wouldn't let her near.*
*Now I'm old and wiser and mostly know my stuff*
*But I still struggle with Easter, I find it really rough.*

*My tummy starts to wobble and I have jelly legs*
*When I see my brother and sisters with all their lovely eggs!*

## WHAT'S HAPPENING HERE?

Just a reminder here... Easter is hard because we want to create the magic and give chocolate treats; and the children crave the sugar and chocolate buzz without understanding why, so they over-indulge. If they know there is chocolate in the house, they WILL hunt it out, they WILL eat it, they *will* be super-fuelled, sick and hyper. It is no good expecting them to exercise control because the higher-order thinking (i.e. executive function – see Chapter 31, 'Memory') that this requires has not yet been built by a consistent and predictable experience.

We are again reminded that the child may be in the grip of very conflicting emotions: there is the memory of the first chocolate – how good that was! On the other hand, there is the vague and hazy idea that this is also connected with pain – a separation, or maybe a different event where something was not what it seemed. The solution? Simple! Eat more chocolate to ease the pain and the fear.

## 🔖 TRY THIS...

- ✓ Give a small gift instead of chocolate, or *with* a small chocolate: for example, an Easter-themed cuddly toy, or a cup with a small chocolate treat. I gave a real bunny one Easter! Get friends and relatives on board. (Difficult, that!)

- ✓ Create Easter treats such as chocolate cake, biscuits, brownies that are sweet but less rocket-fuelled.

- ✓ Have Easter egg hunts following clues but only leading to one egg reward.

✓ Accept what you cannot change. The children will be overexcited. There will be drama. You will wonder why you bother. It's one day. It will pass.

✓ Have empathy – how hard to never have experienced this magic. How sad is that?

✓ Remember – you are building the good memories that heal.

✓ Finally, give self-care. When they collapse into bed exhausted, and you finally manage to sit down for a minute before you follow suit, make sure you save the last treat for yourself!

# 14

# Birthdays

Living with a child who has suffered trauma means that birthdays are not going to be straightforward. As we saw in Chapter 7, 'Christmas', celebration days can be difficult for children to manage. In this chapter, Sarah discovers this and has five birthdays a year to get through! She is beginning to dread these events and the hugely complex feelings and difficult behaviours that emerge.

## ✎ SARAH NAISH: Birthday approaching!

Oh my days! If I hear one more comment about how it's only three weeks until her birthday, I swear I will scream! I know children get excited about their birthdays but this is beyond anything normal.

I was worried at first that Katie would not want to celebrate her birthday. Maybe there were bad memories or even the fact that their birthdays were ignored and went uncelebrated.

It's really hard to manage her excitement when I see the other children getting very wobbly and fidgety about it. I know they won't be able to manage their feelings of jealousy. We are keeping it very low key by just having a few friends and family for tea. This will be the first birthday she is celebrating with us and I want to make it special but I don't want to hype everyone up any more than necessary.

How can I manage all her expectations? It's almost like she thinks her birthday will meet all her emotional needs and put right all the wrongs of the past. But it can't.

## ✎ SARAH NAISH: On the day

Well it wasn't too bad. Katie seemed very happy with her presents although she managed to lose or break three of them before lunch!

The other children alternated between being sulky and argumentative or trying to be Katie's new best friend. It was exhausting!

We were well prepared for the sugar high following the tea party and made sure the trampoline was available with some physical games in the garden.

I am so sad she wasn't born to me though. I know it's selfish but I think of all the birthdays I missed and the actual birth DAY when I wasn't there. I wonder if Katie thinks about that too?

## ⌨ IT'S MY BIRTHDAY! (Katie, soon to be 7 years)

IT'S MY BIRTHDAY in eight days' time and I can't wait!

I want makeup and headphones and a guitar. I can't stop thinking about it, and I'm very excited.

My sisters keep talking about their birthdays and I wish they would shut up. They always have to make everything about them – they're so selfish at times.

I'm being very nice to Mummy as I really want to get all the things I've asked for and hopefully more!

I did write a much longer list of all the things I want, but she said I needed to choose only three.

I'm angry about that but I'll just keep it inside in case she changes her mind and I end up with nothing.

I remember getting nothing when I was little. Sometimes I didn't even realise it was my birthday.

Maybe they didn't feel it was worth celebrating. Perhaps it's not.

Now I feel scared, stupid birthday.

Will I still be having a tea party or has she changed her mind? Who will come? Will I have to share ALL of my cake or will I be able to give a small slice to everyone and keep the rest for myself?

I hope I don't have to share too much of it.

There will probably be chocolate as well. I love chocolate.

I feel a bit fuzzy. Think I'll have a little look around to see if there's any hidden away.

## ⟨⟩ ON THE DAY

Well today is MY big day. I got most of what I wanted and a few extra things. Rosie broke one of my guitar strings, then blamed Sophie. I'm sure she has hidden my new earphones! Mummy said it was my own fault for not putting them somewhere safe.

She always blames me for everything. I wonder if she regrets bringing me here? I wouldn't blame her if she did. I hope she doesn't. I wish I was her 'real' daughter. Birthdays always make me think about the day I was born. Did Jackie ever love me? I don't like these thoughts. More chocolate will help – funny how chocolate makes everything feel better.

## WHAT'S HAPPENING HERE?

We can clearly see the huge and complex emotions that are arising with Sarah and also with Katie.

For Mum (who has learned a thing or two), it is about managing expectations and containing all the emotional content of the day –

this is a big ask, and involves being reflective about her own pain and losses. How different would this have been had it been her own child conceived in her body? And how hard is this for her child?

As well as this, there is the issue of Katie, who will not be able to regulate her strong excitement, and of the other children, who may be triggered by all the attention being centred on Katie and start to act out fears of abandonment and rejection.

For Katie there is a rollercoaster going on. Wildly excited about her birthday, she suddenly thinks of her birth family, which plunges her into a fearful and stressed state – her internal working model has kicked in to remind her to feel that she is not worthwhile. She doesn't deserve anything. No one will remember. Or everyone will try and take her special things from her. She doesn't know what to think. Each thought may trigger an opposite, and in the end it is all too much to manage.

Her siblings (seen through Mum and Katie's eyes) are caught in a fear that they are left out, unseen, invisible. They may have their own survival fears triggered and steal cake and treats due to their expectation of being excluded. They may also become extremely visible (in their behaviour) to avoid falling into their own black spaces where they are forgotten, ignored and completely unimportant.

## 🖋 TRY THIS...

- ✓ Take responsibility for birthday planning away from the child.

- ✓ Keep celebrations small and simple and family orientated.

- ✓ Have one or two meaningful gifts.

- ✓ Avoid overwhelming, noisy environments.

- ✓ Plan carefully and keep your usual structure for the day.

# 15

# The Necessary Lies?

Sometimes we find that vital information is missing from our children's files. Information which would inform behaviours or help parents to piece together their history.

This chapter is not about the child's ability to lie but about how sometimes professionals/society are economical with the truth. This might be due to a desire to present traumatised children in 'the best light' due to the pressing need to find families for children who have suffered trauma. Or, much more worryingly, as in this situation, to conceal mistakes.

## ✎ SARAH NAISH: Missing information

I know our story is unusual in some ways but over the years I have met many therapeutic parents who tell me about how they have been treated so appallingly by a system that is flawed. Our own experience of this was extremely traumatic. We were placed in a situation where I knew vital information about my children's history had been withheld. As a social worker I knew where the gaps were, but no one seemed willing or able to share this essential information with us. I felt the only people who really had the right to know what had happened to them – the truth – were my children.

In the end I had to approach my MP. We went to Westminster, where the Health Minister (along with lots of 'men in suits') ordered the Local Authority to pass on key documents to us. Even then, the Local Authority said we could only sit in a room and read the documents, not take them away. The document contained details of the failings of Social Services and other organisations. All I wanted was the truth.

I sat in the room with a dictaphone and read it out loud. I then went home and typed out the whole thing. This became the document that my children relied on the most, as young adults, to make sense of what had happened to them.

## SARAH NAISH: The lies they tell

Were all the lies necessary? I know Social Services don't think of it as lying. They don't even think of it as being economical with the truth. It makes me so angry. They have worked so hard to hide the extent of abuse and neglect the children suffered. I have had to fight and fight to get to the truth. Why didn't they want me to have this truth? It is the children's truth after all. There has been a lot of 'back covering' going on, where social workers have not wanted to take responsibility for the failings that happened. Failure to protect, failure to act.

Maybe they thought if they told me everything, I wouldn't be able to cope? Wouldn't want the children? Don't they realise that all we really need are the facts. We need help and support to understand what has happened and proper training around how we deal with it. We don't need half-truths and fudging of the central important issues.

The extent to which they went to conceal necessary truths is quite frankly astounding. I had to involve my MP in order to access essential key documents. Documents which talk about my children's early lives and their experiences. Why on earth do Social Services think they have more right to this information than the people it HAPPENED TO?!

I ended up sitting round a big table in the Houses of Parliament, speaking to all the 'men in suits' about my children's 'case'! It's not a 'case'! This is our whole life.

I am fuelled by anger. Consumed by the injustices and indignities my children suffered. All in order to indulge so-called professionals in their back-covering exercise.

I've worked in Social Services. I get it. People make mistakes. We are all human. But for the love of God, give us the facts we need to get our children sorted out! This should not have taken time away from my children. It should not have been a fight.

## THE UNSAID STUFF (Rosie, 8 years)

They know the truth about what happened. They think I've forgotten but I haven't. I remember everything. I saw everything. They haven't told Sarah, so why should I? I bet they are planning something and it won't be good for me.

They didn't get us out. They didn't care about us. Now they keep telling us to trust them. What a joke!

I was angry today. Sarah told me that she knows I'm a brave girl and that the social worker had told her all about me before I came to stay here. I asked her what the stupid social worker had said. Apparently, I'm very brave and grown-up for my age, get on well with adults, always smiling, love shopping, food and playing dressing-up with makeup, etc. Who is she talking about?

This isn't who I am. I hate adults. I only liked shopping with my foster parent so I could get what I wanted. I wore makeup to stop adults treating me like a baby! I do love food though, so at least they got something right!

And I wasn't brave. I couldn't save everyone, so that's not very brave is it?

I NEVER smile...

I need to show Sarah that she's got it wrong. The social worker is stupid and I can't even remember her stupid name! Maybe her name is actually 'Stupid'. Ha ha.

As the day moved on, I got more and more and more angry. Why does she keep calling me 'darling'?

I am not a darling.

I proved it this evening when I told her that I didn't like her stupid dinner (even though I ate it), and stomped off up to my room, slamming all the doors. Sarah wasn't happy at all and shouted very loudly, 'Get back here, young lady, and don't you dare slam the doors like that.'

I feel much better now. At least I don't think she's tricking me any more by pretending that she thinks I'm nice...and brave.

I am not nice...and I wasn't brave. But I AM fierce.

Stupid social worker.

## WHAT'S HAPPENING HERE?

Many families unfortunately experience a situation where important information about the extent of the trauma that a child has endured is either glossed over or deliberately withheld, and this causes immense difficulties for the families, who do not then have the necessary tools to help their children, because they have not been told what happened. This means that the parent and the child are set up to fail.

The parent from the outset will be managing an unknown, will be unable to understand the roots of the adaptive behaviours, and will face confusion and self-doubt as to their ability to manage. The best-case scenario would be that the parent who recognises that there is more going on than meets the eye has to search for the information that they need. The worst-case scenario is that believing the partial truths they have been given, parents do not see the child in the context of their trauma and therefore inappropriately label the child as violent, aggressive, manipulative and lying. A bad child.

This will prevent the empathic response needed to reframe the behaviour and heal the child, reinforcing the negative values that the child places on themselves.

The child loses an opportunity to have a parent who understands their trauma and is able to reframe their behaviour. They are left alone with their secrets and their fears and will continue to play out their adaptive behaviours, driven by their internal working model, which is inadvertently reinforced by the frustrated, exhausted and isolated parent.

Rosie is perfectly aware here that information is being withheld from Sarah but she is too scared to volunteer any information. The only disclosure Mum is likely to see will be demonstrated through Rosie's behaviour.

## ❧ TRY THIS...

✓ Be firm in your expectation of full disclosure about your child. This will allow you to truly give them the experience of being accepted (first) and loved (second) unconditionally with full knowledge of all that they have endured.

✓ Be honest with your child, too. Do not buy in to the 'necessary' lie that birth parents 'did their best', unless you know this to be true. (Read more about this in Chapter 42, 'Honesty'.)

✓ In order to help your child escape from their trauma bonds, you need to know their story.

# 16

# Nonsense Chatter

Nonsense chatter and questions can be very wearing. There is a big difference between nonsense chatter as a normal developmental stage, and the relentless anxiety-based nonsense chatter from traumatised children.

In this chapter Sarah and Peter are finding nonsense chatter and questions a big strain. But why is it happening?

## ✎ SARAH NAISH: My ears are bleeding!

Well, not in real life, but it does actually feel like that. Nonsense questions and chatter I have had today are:

'Why is the carpet purple? Do you like purple? Do I like purple? Can you get purple dogs? I like purple dogs. My aunty had a purple cat...'

On and on and on.

At first, I started answering the questions as I really thought they wanted answers, but I've realised that they don't listen to the answers.

I am sure any perfect parents hearing my children's questions and observations going unanswered will judge me to be a very poor parent.

Well, they haven't heard it from 6.30 am until 7.30 pm, with barely a pause for breath.

Sometimes it makes me feel like my brain is actually shaking. It doesn't seem to matter what I do, the talking carries on incessantly. I've tried answering, not answering, ignoring and explaining that it makes my brain feel wobbly! Nothing has worked so far though.

In the car I put on the radio and turn it up loud to drown it out, but then the talking just gets louder...and more ridiculous!

I know children go through a phase of doing this around 2–3 years old but my lot are ALL still doing it and Rosie is 9 now. Katie and Charley are the 'most skilled!' At least Charley is not far off the right stage for this developmentally!

One day, I think, I will live in a silent house. Then I remember that I used to live in a silent house and all I wanted was for it to be filled with children!

Sometimes, the nonsense chatter can be quite funny as it all comes out without thought. When we went on holiday and landed at the airport, Katie asked, 'Is that a plane?' and 'Are we at the airport?'

I know it's wrong to be sarcastic, and I do try not to be because they don't understand it anyway.

But it's too tempting sometimes!

## ⬚ HERE I AM!! (Charley, 3 years; Katie, 7 years)

*I really can't stop talking 'cos you might forget I'm here.*
*It keeps your focus on me as I bend your weary ear.*
*Lots and lots of nonsense questions.*
*I just switch off from your objections.*

*What's the purpliest purple that you have ever seen?*
*What are we having for dinner and why is the grass green?*
*I'm scared I'll be invisible if I cease to babble on.*
*I need to keep your interest to feel like I belong.*

*I cannot sit here quietly 'cos of wobbles in my belly,*
*So I make lots of noise and I interrupt the telly.*
*What if you don't feed me or make me go away?*
*You'll always know I'm here if I've got lots to say.*

*It's all about survival and making sure you're near.*
*The nonsense in my questions are based within my fear.*
*I hope this drives you crazy and makes you feel insane.*
*Maybe you will see what it's like within MY brain!*

## WHAT'S HAPPENING HERE?

When children are very little, they go through a nonsense chatter stage. Here Charley and Katie have a well-designed strategy. As the children begin to develop independence traits, Mum stops being aware 24/7 (which is what a securely attached baby/toddler is used to), so Charley and Katie in particular seem to need a way to re-focus their mum. They are still not really sure whether otherwise she might just disappear! Their idea of object permanence (i.e. things continue to exist when they are out of sight) is not properly developed.

For children who have experienced developmental trauma, this is part of their brain catching up and also part of them developing an attuned relationship with their parent. The children are working hard to catch up on their developmental tasks.

Katie moved from her foster home to her forever home more recently than her siblings, so her anxiety levels are likely to be even higher – the nonsense chatter is a symptom of this. Mum has already noticed, but hasn't put two and two together: that is, the chatter increases during transitions (car journeys, holidays, etc.).

## ☀ THINK...

✓ The child is seeking a connection with you. This is good. They might also be fighting their rivals (siblings, your partner, your extended family and friends) for your attention. So, as soon as someone else wants to talk to you or – worse – you want to talk to someone else, this triggers immense fear in their brain. You clearly don't love them anymore. They MUST keep your attention. Their survival depends on it. This is not an exaggeration, it is their truth.

## ✿ TRY THIS...

✓ Make a playful response to 'mad' questions.

✓ Accept them – empathise with their wobbly tummy.

✓ Use empathic commentary, wondering aloud, 'I wonder if it feels like I might just disappear if you can't see me. But I promise I always come back.'

✓ Let them know you are not going anywhere. You will always keep them safe. There is enough of you to go round. Or maybe the child feels as if THEY have disappeared when your attention wanders?

✓ Support them to develop confidence and a sense of object permanence, by letting them know you will be back in a moment, like you would if they were tiny. Practise by playing hide and seek and giving a narrative: 'See! I didn't disappear. You can always find me!'

✓ Take mindful moments for yourself – enjoy your favourite tea or coffee, or square of chocolate. Sometimes this gives us the pause we need to reconnect our brain. Enjoy every sip, every mouthful – until you get interrupted again!

# 17

# **Anxiety**

Anxiety is a very common feature in children who have suffered trauma. It underpins many behaviours, such as following the parent and making nonsense chatter (as described in the previous chapter).

In this chapter, as the family settles down, the children are keen to make sure they are safe, and anxieties resurface. Katie in particular is finding her new family environment frightening. Sarah knows this and the strain is beginning to show.

### ✎ SARAH NAISH: Followed

*At the bottom of the stair*
*I turn and find her standing there.*
*Near my bedroom, at the door,*
*She mutely gazes at the floor.*
*In the kitchen, for a while,*
*I know she's waiting for my smile.*

*At every turn and every hour,*
*My shadow follows with a glower.*
*Not for me a cup of tea*
*Without judgement, silently.*

*I feel so bad for needing space*
*Each time I see her anxious face,*
*But I have needs, my fears whirl*
*And settle on this little girl.*

*The teacher always sighs and beckons*
*To tell me all today's transgressions.*
*She is followed, just like me*
*But she goes home at half past three.*
*I take my daughter's hand in mine*
*And tell her everything is fine.*
*It isn't yet, but has to be.*

*One day, my child won't follow me*
*And then I'll wonder where she is.*
*Is she safe or doing drugs?*
*Anxiety transfers, you see,*
*From little ones, to you and me.*

I feel I have a little shadow all the time. I know this is based in anxiety, but it is suffocating. Peter, in particular is really struggling and he works hard to get away. Katie follows him even more, I think, as she is less sure of him. He told her to 'leave him alone' yesterday. Yes great, thanks for that, Pete. Just took me a few hours to get her back on an even keel...

## FOLLOWING (Katie, 7 years)

*'Mummy, where are you going?'*
*'Off to the loo.'*
*'Please don't leave me, I want to come too.'*
*'I'm coming straight back, I said that I will.'*
*I don't quite believe, and I can't sit still.*

*She leaves the room and I think she's gone.*
*For ever, I'm left, I just can't go on.*
*She's not coming back and I think I might die.*
*I stand outside the loo but I ain't gonna cry!*

*Wherever she goes I must follow her there.*
*Right at her heel as she climbs every stair.*
*It's scary without her as I climb in my bed.*
*What if she leaves me, what if she's dead!*

*I need to be near her to make sure she knows*
*I need more than showers and books, toys and clothes.*
*I need her to see me whatever she's doing,*
*To not turn around when she does all that cooking.*

*I know what to do: I'll ask lots of questions.*
*I can't sit and wait as it feels like rejection.*
*Maybe she'll forget me, not realise I'm there.*
*Jackie would shout or turn around and swear.*

*I call out her name throughout the day.*
*I can't be alone and I don't like to play.*
*I hang onto her leg when she takes me to school.*
*The other kids laugh 'cos they think I'm a fool.*

*I hit out and punch them and call them all names.*
*They don't understand me or let me join in their games.*
*I want to go home and be with my mum.*
*What if she's left me, what if she's gone!*

*Mum's there at the gate at the end of the day.*
*The teacher's unhappy as I 'must' learn to play.*
*Mum turns and hugs me and tells me I'm safe.*
*She's not gonna leave me and says that I'm brave.*

*She knows that I'm scared and I don't know why,*
*But we'll figure it out, together we'll try,*
*To work out a way to help me believe*
*That she ain't giving up and she's not gonna leave.*

*She'll be there in the morning and last thing at night.*
*She'll be there when I'm scared,*
*When I hit out and fight.*
*She's not gonna leave me,*
*She's not gonna go,*
*But I can't believe that. It just isn't so.*

## WHAT'S HAPPENING HERE?

Among the longstanding strain of anxiety in the relationship, we also start seeing the first signs of Mum being able to reassure her child, and the child beginning to accept it, even though she can't believe it. This is a stage which needs to be gone through with each child in different ways: the gradual lessening of anxiety and beginnings of trust.

The child's anxiety and, in fact, terror at separation is a sign that Mum is becoming important, but this causes intense anxiety as the child has only experienced that people who are supposed to care for you hurt you, shout at you, and get rid of you. The child who is used to feeling invisible *has* to make sure that the adult is available and aware of them at all times. This is deeply ingrained survival behaviour and is also completely developmentally appropriate for a child who suffered trauma at a very young age. Think about a toddler – they get scared and seek or call out for their adult attachment figure all the time. This kind of checking continues until a child is old enough to remember to go and seek out the parent. In a securely attached child this will be in place to an extent by 3 years old, although the child may still be very needy.

For the parent this is unbelievably hard. Your child is being demanding and needy 24/7 – you can't even get to the loo! Never mind have time for yourself! What more are you supposed to do? This is so hard and not what you expected.

A part of a child's normal developmental stage is that of the toddler shadow (around 1 year onwards) when they can and will follow you round and call for you all the time. This can continue for a few years! If your child has had an interrupted development, they will need to do this no matter what age they really are, as they need the experience of always knowing you are there to build security and trust.

## ⚡ TRY THIS...

✓ Take time for you. Build it into your timetable as children love routine.

✓ Find ways to practise calming techniques and use whatever time you can squeeze in (e.g. when the children are at school) to put yourself first.

✓ Breathing exercises can also really help in the moment – pause, take deep breaths and count to ten. This can help you to retain your therapeutic stance and help you not to step into an emotional response.

✓ Try to stay positive. Remember the child is using the only attachment strategies they have to try to engage with you.

# 18

# Exhaustion (Compassion Fatigue)

Sometimes it can seem relentless. Parenting traumatised children is hard work and often unrewarding. Eighteen months after reunification, when Rosie and Katie joined the family, the family is starting to have serious problems, culminating in Peter leaving home.

## ✎ SARAH NAISH: Breaking up

Even though Peter had been the driving force behind reuniting all the children, by the time they had all been together for 18 months, the cracks were not so much cracks as chasms! Peter spent a lot of his time at work, doing 48-hour shifts. He seemed to prefer long shifts in children's homes to being at home with his children (and me).

I realised that I was doing near enough everything with the children and that Peter had withdrawn from all of them apart from Charley. The children relied on me completely and went everywhere with me.

When Peter was at home, he withdrew into computer games or meeting friends. I could not see what was happening under my nose and had no energy to address it.

Over the last few weeks he became more and more remote. I thought he was avoiding me, but it turns out it was the children. At this point we had adopted the youngest three but Rosie and Katie were not yet legally adopted.

One day Peter told me he could not proceed with the adoption of the older girls and said I needed to choose between him and them. He said he couldn't connect to Rosie and Katie. He suggested that I 'send them back.' I was not sure where 'back' was.

Peter left the family and refused to see the children again.

### SARAH NAISH: Doubts

The thing is, although I am angry, I also get it. It *is* draining and sometimes I feel very disconnected from one or the other. Maybe I am just a bad person? Maybe I am just not cut out for parenting. I just don't seem to have that natural 'mum love' sometimes. To be honest, at times I don't even like one of them. There, I've said it. I am a dreadful person and I can never say that out loud to another human being.

I stand and look at one of the children when they are sleeping and pray to God to help me find enough love in my heart for this child. It just isn't there.

This is relentless, exhausting, thankless, depressing and grinding. I have never felt more hopeless in my life. I have heard about post-adoption depression and I wonder if this might have something to do with it?

This isn't how I thought it would be; the behaviours, the unkindness, the never-ending arguments, washing, fighting and low-level sniping, the sneakiness, the stealing and lying. Surely it should not be this hard? What am I doing wrong?

I can't tell anyone. They will just say, 'Well you chose to adopt.' Or even worse, they might say the same as Peter. No one gets it. I am alone, not coping, not supported, understood or listened to in any way.

But I'm not giving up.

## ಬ DADDY'S GONE (Any Child)

*Daddy's forgotten how to smile,*
*And laugh,*
*And help,*
*And play.*
*Daddy couldn't stay, you see,*
*And so he's gone away.*

*Daddy, he got really tired.*
*Well, Mummy's tired too,*
*But Daddy is too tired to care.*
*Mummy won't leave you,*
*But Mummy feels so tired inside,*
*(Don't worry, I won't say).*
*I'll think about how bad it was*
*When Daddy went away.*

## ಬ I'M LOSING YOU, I KNEW I WOULD! (William, 5 years)

I'm scared. Something is different about Mummy. She still replies to me if I ask her a question, but her answers are very short. Her tone of voice is weird. There is no singing. Mummy always used to sing. I follow her everywhere just in case she leaves like Daddy did. I don't miss him, I'm used to people leaving. It's probably my fault that he left anyway. I wonder if Mummy misses him. I don't want Mummy to leave.

## ⬚ WEIRD MUMMY (Sophie, 4 years)

I'm scared. Mummy's eyes don't look right. They're very dark and it feels like she's looking through me rather than at me. It feels as though she's not really there. I hope she hasn't been swapped with a different Mummy, perhaps one who looks like her. She speaks like a robot. It makes me feel very wobbly. I needed a cuddle today. She gave me one but she was very stiff and the cuddle didn't last more than a second. I think it was a pretend cuddle.

Mummy's quiet. I don't know what's wrong. What have I done? Will my dinner be on time?

Will she leave like Daddy did or will she make me leave? I don't know what to do and it's making all my wobbly feelings come out. Mummy isn't even shouting at Rosie.

I bet Daddy went because I am so horrible. He must have realised. Stupid Daddy.

I'd feel better if Mummy shouted. At least I'd know she was normal again. I think she may have stopped loving me. I don't blame her. I don't deserve to be loved anyway. Perhaps I'll start packing my bags and go to live with a new mummy.

## WHAT'S HAPPENING HERE?

Two words: 'compassion fatigue'.

## ⬚ THINK...

- ✓ Have you ever felt that disconnect? As if you do not even like your child? As though you cannot connect to them?

- ✓ Do you feel that you cannot continue, or that you are isolated?

✓ You are not alone! Compassion fatigue is the largest contributor to family breakdowns, and also the reason for many more relationship breakdowns when one partner chooses their children, then carries on alone.

In the parent and child perspectives above we can feel the exhaustion, hopelessness and flattening of emotional response of Sarah, who is also shattered by the desertion of Peter and the way that the children, who are immensely triggered by the disruption, assume responsibility – they always knew everything horrible that happens is due to their own badness. This triggers an expectation on the child's part that they will need to leave, and in turn additional stress is placed on Sarah as the children, in expectation of rejection and overwhelming stress, display hostile and rejecting behaviours which is their only way of dealing with intense, unbearable emotional pain.

The first-ever research into compassion fatigue, relating to parents who are re-parenting traumatised children, was carried out at Bristol University by the Hadley Centre for Adoption and Foster Care Studies, and was commissioned by Sarah Naish (Fostering Attachments Ltd). The research describes compassion fatigue as a result of the emotional, physical and biological demands on a parent who is living with a traumatised child.

The main factors are:

- Burnout: This is physical and emotional exhaustion.

- Secondary traumatic stress: The connection between the parent and the child is so great that the parent suffers symptoms which mirror their child's – fear, intrusive thoughts and isolation.

- Lack of compassion satisfaction: We are enabled to continue by the positive emotional feedback we get, but this may be absent.

These factors were found to be higher in foster parents (and by extension likely to be so in adoptive parents) than in any other helping professions where compassion fatigue is recognised.

## ♟ REMEMBER...

✓ Traumatised children often cannot show empathy or engage in positive interactions. They did not have an attuned adult to help them understand the positive effect of simple attachment interactions where the pleasure of eliciting a response from each other enables both sides to overcome the many obstacles of 24-hour care needed by a newborn or small child. Furthermore, the intense feelings generated by positive interactions are scary, and may lead to anxious rejecting behaviour.

✓ We need to remember that our child cannot help themselves, and we can help them by having connected moments that can build awareness. This means 5–10 minutes of playing with them – for example, building experiences when we are sure they can manage.

✓ During times of stress, including feelings of disconnection, we have to find our comfort, support and validation else-where – for instance, among others who understand our lives such as sympathetic friends, family or peer support groups.

✓ Compassion fatigue *can* be overcome. It requires, above all, having the comfort and support of an understanding peer group or a place to celebrate your triumphs, but also getting support, help and hugs from those people who understand. The National Association of Therapeutic Parents was formed specifically to help parents to overcome compassion fatigue by providing peer support and listening circles. Find out more at www.naotp.com.

## ✎ SARAH NAISH: Being a single parent

After Peter left, I tried without success, to encourage him to see the children. I realised that I had been very used to doing nearly everything with the children, taking them all out with me and generally making sure their needs were met. It was only after he was gone that I realised the extent to which this had happened.

Being a single parent had benefits as well as disadvantages. There was only one set of rules, and it was easier to keep track of who said what when. I hardly had time to grieve the ending of my marriage, especially as I also now had to deal with the children's loss and the practical side of getting divorced.

I did not see a particular increase in the children's behaviours, apart from Katie whose anxiety was more pronounced. She needed lots of reassurance that Peter had not left because of her.

As Peter and I had adopted the youngest three children, but not yet adopted Rosie and Katie, I had to start the assessment process for adopting them all over again, but this time as a single adopter.

I encountered huge resistance to this and ended up writing my own matching report for the adoption Panel to show the importance of the children's relationships with each other, and blossoming attachments to me. I felt it would have been devastating to separate the children again.

At Panel it was unanimously agreed that I would keep all five children and I moved swiftly to get the adoption order in the court. It was only once this was granted, when Rosie and Katie were 10 and 8 years respectively, that we all began to feel a bit more secure.

# 19

# Hypochondria

It can be astonishing how children from a traumatic background can be so ill, then suddenly bounce back! You might almost think they were making it up. It is commonplace for children to misinterpret feelings of pain or illness, and equally as common for children to instinctively use the parent's need to care as a way of making sure they are nurtured. After all, they missed so much.

This can be extremely challenging for the parents, especially where there is a very high frequency of 'illness' which turns out to be nothing at all.

## ✎ SARAH NAISH: Ill again

I have actually lost count of the number of times the school has phoned me up to tell me either Rosie or Katie are 'ill'.

I swear they must actually be the healthiest children in the school, but you would never think it. They are so good at acting out other people's illnesses.

Yesterday the school phoned me to say Katie had been sick. They hadn't actually seen the sick, so I knew it hadn't really happened. A tummy bug is going round the school, so Katie wanted to join in. I suppose she wanted to be home with me. Again. I am sure the school thinks I am a nasty parent, but

I know when she is faking it and she is so good at turning on those puppy dog eyes.

Then today... Well, Rosie really took the biscuit! School phoned to say she had 'fallen over'. I tried wriggling out of it and being busy, but as they were threatening to call an ambulance and saying she couldn't walk, etc. I thought I had better go up and sort it out.

So the TA [teaching assistant] pushed Rosie out of the school in a wheelchair. Rosie was smiling happily. Something in me just snapped and I screeched, 'Get out of that wheelchair now and walk.' The look on the TA's face was priceless when the miracle occurred.

Two hours later I phoned the school to say Rosie was happily playing hopscotch with me on her nearly broken leg.

This so draining and frustrating! The worst part is that people just keep falling for it all the time. I find it easier when I say to the children, 'I see what you did there. I think you needed extra cuddle time.' At least that feels more honest.

All the time though, I am being blamed and judged by people who genuinely believe that my children are always ill!

## ⭐ KATIE (8 years)

I quite like being ill as it means I get to spend more time at home with Mummy. I miss her when I'm at school. I worry that she may have forgotten about me and might not pick me up at the end of the day. That would be really scary.

Also, the teachers are really nice to me when I'm poorly. They call me 'Sweetheart' and let me lie down in the medical room. It's very nice in the medical room. There are pictures of cartoon frogs on the wall and even a little green blanket on the trolley-bed thing. I like blankets. I've also learned to pretend to make myself sick and can even do all the sounds.

I sometimes get Mummy to believe it too and she comes to pick me up early.

Rosie got into big trouble though, as she's not as good at pretending.

## ROSIE (10 years)

Well today did not go well. I fell over in the playground at school – I really did fall over, or maybe someone deliberately tripped me up! I'll ask my friends tomorrow. Anyway, the lunchtime supervisors all ran over to me as I was making quite a lot of noise. Mrs Gordon was a bit worried and said my leg looked like it was lying at a funny angle and she hoped it wasn't broken. I really liked all the attention and so just went along with it.

Then they called Sarah and told her I needed to go to the hospital.

'Oh dear,' I thought. 'I wonder what will happen when Sarah finds out I'm only pretending!'

When Sarah eventually arrived (she took quite a while to get there), Mrs Harding wheeled me out to her in a wheelchair. I loved being in the wheelchair – it was great fun, almost like being in a pushchair.

I put on my biggest smile when I saw her, but she had that terrible 'STOP IT NOW' look on her face. She screamed at me to get out of the wheelchair and walk. I got out and walked. It was one of those moments when I was out before I'd even had a chance to think about it! Mrs Harding had a big shocked look on her face. I had a sinking feeling in my tummy and my head felt all hot.

I soon felt better though, and in no time at all, I was playing out in the garden.

Sarah said it looked like a miracle had happened.

## WHAT'S HAPPENING HERE?

It is much easier to think of Rosie and Katie's behaviour as 'attention needing' rather than 'attention seeking'.

Children aren't stupid. The best way to get lots of attention very quickly is to be ill. Maybe they really *do* feel ill, or 'wobbly' but they lack the necessary skills to interpret or express what is happening in their body due to faulty neuroception. Have you ever felt 'a bit odd' and not been able to explain that?

When you are ill, you get sympathy, cuddles, lots of concerned faces. It feels really nice to be at the centre of all the fuss. What's not to like, really? Children like to have a day off school, some nice quiet time with a parent, no sharing of Mummy or Daddy, no arguments over the TV, no arguments over what you want to eat. Perfect!

It's also a way for children to stay safe. If they are at home, they have avoided a transition and are keeping themselves safe.

## ♀ REMEMBER...

- ✓ It is important to let children know that we know. But, as in our example, we must also let them know that we also understand the underlying reasons, and that we will care for them and meet their needs: 'I see what you did there. I think you needed some more cuddle time!'

## ♀ TRY THIS...

- ✓ Let the child know they do not need to be ill to get your care or your attention.

- ✓ Try to set up a routine so that each child gets some one-to-one time, each child on a different night.

✓ Do insist on 'me' time for yourself. That's a huge burden of care, so make sure that your self-care is sufficient to enable you to continue.

# 20

# **Wee and Poo**

Many traumatised children have issues with wee and poo. They may be delayed or there might be much more deep-seated issues. This can put a big strain on any family.

Now we are a few months after Peter has left the family. William, Sophie and Charley have been home for just over three years, and Rosie and Katie for two. Some serious issues are arising which seem linked to the children's trauma. These are causing daily difficulties in the home. Sarah is feeling under siege, but why is this happening?

✎ SARAH NAISH: The horrible poo and stinky wee

When did my house start smelling like a toilet? It's so long ago now I can't remember.

I expected there to be poo and wee issues when Sophie, Charley and William were very little. They all came to me in nappies, and William was nearly 4 years old! I stupidly believed that with my childcare background I could easily sort this out given a few nice weather days.

How wrong I was!

Charley likes to hold on to her poos as long as possible. This leads to some interesting moments, usually when we are out and surrounded by the maximum number of people, when the poo just can't be held any longer! Last week we were at the bird zoo having a lovely time when I noticed the usual protrusion sticking out from the back of her leggings.

At home she will leave the poos in places for me to find. I honestly have no idea what that is all about. The dogs usually alert me to the smell (luckily) as I think I've almost become used to it.

William is basically always wet. We have used pull-ups a fair bit, but then the doctor said he wouldn't feel the sensation so it was better to let him wear normal clothes. The doctor didn't have to do the washing...

The problem is that I am changing him literally every 30 minutes and I swear he is entirely unaware when he does it. It can happen a lot when he is overexcited or scared but as that's most of the time, well...

Sometimes he wets the bed and then just lies in it. I have tried showing him that Mummy isn't cross, etc. but nothing seems to work. He basically just wants to lie in a wet bed.

Sometimes he wees in the bin in his room and hides it under the bed. I worry that one day I won't find it. I've tried asking him why, but he just stares at me. Maybe he's scared to go to the toilet.

I am so thankful that, so far, we don't have many of these issues with Rosie and Katie (crosses fingers, touches lots of wood). Just the odd night-time accident with Katie, and Rosie is 'quite fine, thank you very much'!

I am at such a loss.

## CHARLEY'S PICNIC (4 years)

Oh dear, I've pooed my pants.

Mummy said we were going out for a lovely day at the bird zoo. We took a picnic.

My tummy was all wishy-washy like a washing machine and my face was all hot.

I didn't tell Mummy about the wishy-washy feeling. I don't tell her anything. I haven't told her that my wellies are too tight either and pinching my toes. I like wearing my wellies, even when Mummy says it's too hot.

William smells of wee. He often smells of wee. I think he likes wee.

Mummy has laid all the food out on the picnic blanket. Rosie is being very rude and Katie is helping Mummy. Sophie hasn't stopped moaning. Mummy looks a bit pink and her voice sounds a bit different. I don't like it when everyone is so loud and I don't like Mummy's pink face!

I want to go home NOW. I don't say anything, though. I just do a big fat poo.

Mummy's face is now turning from pink to red. I wonder why?

## WILLIAM'S WEE (7 years)

I like the smell of wee. I'm used to it. It's like a warm hug when I feel wobbly.

At night I'm scared and often wake up in a wet bed. I don't mind but I know it makes Mummy sigh a lot. She says it's OK, but I don't think it is.

Sometimes I wee the wobbly feelings out in the laundry basket or on the floor. I feel a bit better for a while, and then I feel bad again so I hide the wet stuff.

Mummy said she thinks this is 'sad' wee. I think she may be right. Happy wees go in the toilet. I don't think I do many happy wees.

## WHAT'S HAPPENING HERE?

There are several issues happening here.

The first is around failure of 'interoception'. In other words, there is not much understanding of the physical sensation of needing the loo. If no one ever noticed you doing 'the potty dance' and gave you the information that you look like you need to go to the toilet, it's hard to make the connection. If no one noticed you straining and crouching, and encouraged you to poo on the loo, if you don't have words for those feelings and have never been praised for appropriate actions, then these things need to be supported, just like a toddler would be.

The second reason is hard to understand, but is very common. For the child who has suffered severe neglect, it may be that in the middle of their sensory deprivation the sensation of warm wee is really very pleasant. The smell is at least a stimulation, a diversion. It may provide comfort where there is no other comfort to be found. Maybe it feels good to poo, to have the soft squishy feeling. It might become a plaything, a substance to explore the properties of in the absence of appropriate stimulation. This sounds absurd, but some children are abandoned in their cots, with no stimulation, and their needs barely met. They may survive but carry the trauma scars. Also let us remember that we reach for the familiar – it is comforting. So, the smell of wee and poo can even seem familiar and safe when your world is changing. There is no concept for the young child that it is a change for the better. It is scary, confusing and impossible to interpret.

Wee and poo are also ways that children show us their trauma. This is especially true of trauma that occurred before the child had language skills (pre-verbal trauma). At this stage, memory is stored in the body. Children who cannot express their trauma show us by their actions and their bodily functions: poo, wee, sick, spit, hitting or cutting (self-harm).

Lastly, we evacuate our bowels and urinate when faced with immense survival stress. This is what happens to Charley. When she is faced with overwhelming and unusual stimulation (a picnic and a visit to the bird zoo), together with the trauma-based reactions of her siblings, and her inability to put her feelings into words, as well as a sense of dread as Mum seems to sigh and get pinker, her body lets go of the accumulated poo that she has been holding in. She may not realise that everyone needs to poo. She could hold on to poo through fear that it is her insides coming out. But in the end the body takes over.

Of course, when children realise the power of poo and wee to cause upset and disgust, their need to control and prove their 'wrongness' may mean that this is also like a weapon to be used under stress.

## ·Ö· THINK...

- ✓ Think about your child's early history, and the developmental tasks that may not have been supported.

- ✓ Some biological children also have wee and poo issues, sometimes linked to disorders and diagnoses that also indicate developmental issues such as autism spectrum disorder (ASD).

- ✓ However old your child is, if they have not learned sphincter control, or if they control this in adverse ways, they need support and help to recognise the signs of their body and to choose to manage differently.

- ✓ Sometimes children consider their own poo and wee as inner 'badness'. They need to get these bodily fluids out to show you their badness, or they may feel they need to hide this 'badness' (which we call 'trauma').

✓ As they grow older, children may display similar behaviours relating to menstruation: the concealment or display of sanitary towels, etc.

# 21

# Hypervigilance

Children who have experienced severe trauma are constantly on the alert for danger without even knowing it. They may have had to watch and listen very carefully to protect themselves in dangerous situations, so these senses become very well developed.

The children in Sarah's family have had long periods where they were left alone with frightening, unsafe adults approaching them. They are therefore watchful and tense.

This is what it looks and feels like...

## ✎ SARAH NAISH: Stalked

I think there is a difference between being watched and being stalked!

If I go into the kitchen, five little pairs of eyes watch me all the time. They watch where I'm going, what I'm doing, and seem to want to try to see inside my head to see what I am thinking! If I even move the tiniest thing, three of them will comment on the fact that it was moved. If something has changed position in the car, everyone has to remark on that. It drives me up the wall!

They remember everywhere we ate anything they liked, and they remember every single tiny little event where anything happened which was unusual. Sometimes I feel like I am living my life under a microscope! It drives me MAD!

At times, William's eyes are as big as saucers. Usually he looks frozen at the same time. It feels like he is fixated in terror and I can't reach him. I never really know what he is seeing.

At school the teachers have noticed that William struggles to recognise people if they have changed clothes. Non-school-uniform days, or dressing-up days are a big no-no! Last week I had to go and sit under the desk with him to help him get out. It turned out that his teacher had changed her glasses and he didn't recognise her.

Last week we went to Brewster's for tea. When Brewster the Bear came in, William screamed and hid under the table. He was terrified. After he came out, he literally sat rigid with his eyes fixed on the door.

We won't be going back there again,

I understand why they have to keep a lookout for anything that might be dangerous but I'm so tired that I am still one of the things that has to be watched so closely.

It also means I can't get away with anything. If I sigh quietly, really quietly, they hear it and watch me even more carefully.

## WATCHING (William, 7 years)

*They think that I don't see them,*
*But I don't miss a thing.*
*I sit here in the corner*
*And let it all sink in.*

*At times she moves too quickly,*
*That look upon her face,*
*I tense up all my body,*
*I look for my escape.*

*I even feel her eyeballs*
*Drilling through my head,*
*But when her back is turned towards me,*
*It fills me with sick dread.*

*I hear her when she sighs,*
*Looking like she's done,*
*The shaking of her head*
*Makes me want to run.*

*I heard her tell the teacher*
*That's she's not sure what to do.*
*The teacher said she likes me*
*But she hasn't got a clue.*

*Sometimes in the playground*
*Someone bangs the gate.*
*The noise makes me wobbly*
*My insides start to shake.*

*The teacher tries to trick me,*
*Pretending she's not changed.*
*I don't recognise her,*
*But she still knows my name.*

*Mummy says she's worried,*
*I heard her telling Dad.*
*She thinks I have a problem,*
*Perhaps I'm very sad.*

*I hear those conversations*
*When they think I'm fast asleep,*
*Listening at their door*
*With slippers on my feet.*
*Ready for my exit*
*In case I need to run*

*If someone tries to 'get me'*
*Or the monster says he'll come.*
*At night I'm filled with terror,*
*Keep my feet up off the floor,*
*I lay there like a statue,*
*Staring at the door.*
*My breath sounds very loud,*
*There's banging in my head*
*Will I wake up in the morning*
*In an unfamiliar bed?*
*I listen to the sounds*
*That others say aren't there,*
*But I know every floorboard*
*That creaks upon the stairs.*
*These noises are so scary,*
*Like someone's breaking in.*
*I hold my breath inside me*
*But in my head, I scream.*

## WHAT'S HAPPENING HERE?

It is so hard for parents to live under this intense scrutiny. To understand, we have to take the perspective of the child, who has known the intense stress of their very survival being at risk. Looking at Sarah's family, William has lived in terror during a significant period of his life, during which he was powerless. In order to survive, he learned to read tiniest signals contained in body language, facial expression and movement and to respond to these stimuli.

Some of the child's stress stimuli will involve senses other than the visual: for example, sounds – tone of voice, doors slamming; or smells – alcohol on the breath, a particular scent. Movement will also be interpreted – is this a hostile or a friendly stance?

When other babies and toddlers were learning to explore in a safe and nurturing environment which promoted developmental tasks and allowed socialisation, exploration and learning, William was learning only how to survive, how to stay alive.

## Fight/flight/stress response

Imagine the reality of the child who is so used to danger that they cannot turn this mechanism off. Their internal working model informs them that adults are extremely dangerous and unpredictable. The smallest departure from the norm triggers the amygdala (a region in the brain that detects threats and prepares the body to respond) and the fight/flight response is initiated. This causes dilation of the pupils – hence 'eyes like saucers' – and oxygenated blood to flow to the heart and muscles in preparation for fighting or running away.

This occurs before the child is conscious of what they are responding to. In this state, their ability to think and reason has been lost – time spent thinking can decrease the chances of survival, so the thinking brain is offline.

Such a response can feel like a child is reacting to us in a personal way. However, in reality it is the child's hardwired response to life as a result of the experiences that have formed their brain's cortex. The cortex is the part of the brain which makes connections, linking all of our functions and holding our individual ideas and thoughts – it is the thinking and responding part of the brain. We also have a prefrontal cortex which enables us to organise, plan, control impulses and understand cause and effect; this region is severely affected by early trauma giving rise to difficulties in all these areas. In these children, the only areas of the brain that are fully activated are the areas necessary for survival.

Once we understand this, we can start to think about how to make use of the brain's ability to activate new areas of the brain and forge new neuronal connections (called 'plasticity') to calm the child and start the long job of changing the internal working model.

## ⚡ TRY THIS...

✓ Use empathy to name their need and curiosity to discuss this. For example, noticing a child is worried when you pick them up from school: 'You look as though you are feeling a bit wobbly. I wonder if you had a tricky time today? School can be tough sometimes! Remember, I can help you if you would like me to.'

✓ Give them a narrative: 'I am just moving this because...'

✓ Use *consistency*, *predictability* and *reliability* (timetables, routines, designated seats, crockery, etc.).

✓ Take baby steps when exploring new activities.

✓ Find a safe place to explore your own emotional response so that you can maintain your therapeutic parenting equilibrium.

✓ Give warnings about sudden movements and noises where possible.

# 22

# Meeting All Those Needs

Sarah is starting to question why she decided to adopt such a large group of children. It was never the plan to be a single parent to five children! It was not a straightforward decision but there are benefits *and* disadvantages.

✎ SARAH NAISH: Sometimes I wonder!

People sometimes ask me why I adopted so many children. Sometimes I wonder too! It was essential to keep all the children together as they had suffered so much and lost so much. I didn't want them to lose any more. I also thought that, whatever we decided to do, there was no changing the fact that these children are siblings and will have a lifelong bond.

The decision itself was not a complicated one, but the amount I have had to pay in personal sacrifice has been more – much more – than I anticipated.

The hardest thing to deal with is the constant undercurrent of arguing and tension. Sometimes I do actually wonder if they love each other at all. Did I do the right thing? Would they have been happier in separate homes?

At times the hatred which is on the surface is so strong. If they have a disagreement or fight over something, if I didn't intervene there could be serious damage done! I try not to referee as this makes things worse but I literally cannot leave the room without one of them starting to poke the other or starting sneaky punching!

The control issues are very prevalent too. I have to make sure that I am always the one 'in charge', otherwise one of the older girls is very quick to step in and 'help'. They block each other's way by standing at the bottom of the stairs or in doorways.

Rosie is very strong and focused and I admire that in her. She also has compassion but doesn't realise that yet.

Katie is still very clingy and anxious but she has such a kind heart and will do anything for anyone.

William tends to 'go with the flow', but I do worry how it will affect him in later life with four very bossy sisters controlling his every move!

Sophie is our little hand-grenade child, working hard to keep the focus off her. She is very endearing and everyone's friend.

Charley is a little fire-cracker who is not afraid to speak her mind.

They all have different traits, strengths and weaknesses, but there is always competition to be 'the best'. It's exhausting reassuring them all constantly that I love them all the same.

## I AM THE BOSS (Rosie, 10 years)

I get really cross when Sarah tries to boss us all about. She acts like she knows everything about my sisters and brother, but she doesn't!

I had to take care of all of them when I was little. I made sure they got food. I even stood in the doorway to stop Kevin from hurting them. I remember sneaking a bit of sausage into William when he was in the cot. Why does she think it's her job to sort us all out now?

Perhaps it's because the little ones came here before me and now she thinks they're hers!

I know them better than anyone else. Sarah doesn't even realise that Sophie starts lots of arguments when she's not looking. Yesterday, Sophie told Katie that she wasn't going to get her pocket money as her bedroom was still messy. Katie started to cry. I felt sorry for her, so I punched Sophie. As usual she screamed so loudly that Sarah came running in. When I tried to explain, she wouldn't even listen. She really gets on my nerves sometimes. I hadn't even hit Katie that hard.

Charley is very annoying. She's had everything but still doesn't shut up asking for stuff all the time. I think she's a spoilt brat. She didn't even live with Jackie and Kevin, so what has she got to complain about? I'm angry about that. I feel a bit better after I get her into trouble. I need to take extra special care of William – I don't trust any adult to look after him properly. I know why but I'm not saying.

It's really hard being the eldest. There are lots of times when I'm worried that we won't all get what we need or that someone will be selfish and take everything, especially food.

## WHAT'S HAPPENING HERE?
### Parentification

It is so hard to imagine as a parent, but Rosie's experiences have made her take on a parenting role. She is the oldest and was the younger children's protector through unbelievable experiences even though she was not much more than a baby herself. She knows what parents can do to children; she is not about to trust anyone. Rosie's internal working model and the amount of self-esteem she has depend on her fulfilling that role. Also, as is always the case, she has to control her environment to survive.

## Re-traumatisation and trauma bonds

Bryan Post[1] 'states that a trauma bond (sibling rivalry at its worst) is due to a 'life or death dynamic'.

Children in the same family where there is neglect may survive at the expense of each other. If there is not enough food to go round, for example, then the fact that your siblings need to eat threatens your survival. Rosie in her parentified role is trying to ensure the needs of the youngest are met. Siblings in an abusive household form trauma bonds with each other. In its simplest form, this is based on the bonding that occurs as a result of survival after a traumatic experience; however it will be coloured by individual relationships and roles. These may include rescuing each other but may also include victimisation of a scapegoat, assuming a maternal role, and reinforcing old patterns of behaviour due to stress.

Children who come from the same family still have a different experience according to the roles that they assume, which might be parent, scapegoat, 'golden child', baby, etc.

It is hard to shake off these roles which are how you identify yourself, and harder to shake off the bonds and neurological pathways formed by hard and repeated experience.

---

1  See https://postinstitute.com. The Post Institute was founded by Bryan Post who is an adult child from care and a foster carer. The Post Institute provides education solutions and support to anyone who is working with a child suffering from complex trauma.

## ☀ THINK...

- ✓ Which roles do your children fulfil?

- ✓ Can you help them to identify these and move on?

- ✓ Remember that this will be an individual task for each one and may take years to achieve.

# 23

# No Friends

Many children who have been unable to form a safe and loving bond with a main caregiver are unable to then use those skills to form friendships with other children. This is very difficult for parents and children and there is often not very much the parent can do.

Sarah's adopted children don't seem to be able to make friends very easily and this is worrying for Sarah. It is sad and confusing for both parties.

✎ SARAH NAISH: Everyone's friend

I feel so sad for Charley. She tries hard to make friends, but she almost consumes them with her need! As an outsider I can clearly see the new friend feels suffocated.

I've tried everything. If I invite them round they seem to last an even shorter length of time.

The pattern seems to be the same with all the children, to be honest. They start talking (incessantly) about the potential friend. I always start worrying when there seems to be this one topic of conversation.

With Charley, she soon starts giving away lots of her possessions to the child in question, in order to try to impress them. Usually I see a bit of an increase in things going missing from home as well.

Everything seems to go great for about three to four weeks, and Charley is really happy, almost on a high. Then the other child starts backing off.

At this point Charley gets angry with me and blames everybody else around her. I have tried talking to her about being a little bit more relaxed and casual with her friendships, but she's just unable to do that. Then we start the whole cycle again.

I am really at a loss to know how to help my poor little lonely girl develop a real friendship. Last week, the former 'new best friend' just turned on her heel and walked away. She was calling Charley a 'weirdo' but, to be honest, she looked scared. I hope Charley isn't bullying anyone. I am glad I adopted the children together and they have sibling relationships (of a kind); but what if they only ever have those kinds of stressed connections? I fear for their future relationships.

I would really love the friendships to work out. How I long to have people round for tea. Maybe the mums could come in as well and have a coffee with me?

This doesn't happen. This never happens. The parents look at me with a mixture of sympathy and exasperation. They just want to protect their child from mine. I can't really blame them, but I do.

## BE MY FRIEND (Charley, 6 years)

I haven't got any friends (just pretend I have). They won't let me join in their games and they call me names. I usually end up punching them. I always get the blame, even though they start it. I think Mummy believes me sometimes, but school never does. The parents always give me dirty looks in the playground. I never get an invitation to their parties.

I want lots and lots of friends. Everyone else has lots of friends, except for Ginny of course. Ginny is a bit weird and people call her names. I sit and watch her during playtime. She seems OK to me, but I can't be her friend as the other kids would laugh at me. I absolutely HATE people laughing at me. It makes me really angry. I go all red and I get a buzzing sound in my ears.

Recently, I tried to make friends with Amy and her group. Everybody loves Amy. She's really pretty and her mum gives her anything she wants.

I wish I was Amy.

I borrowed a nice necklace from home and gave it to Amy, hoping she would be my friend. She was for a week then wouldn't speak to me again. I don't know why. Perhaps she thinks I'm like Ginny.

Maybe I am. Ruby and Jess pick on Ginny. Maybe I could be their friend and laugh at her as well.

I can't though, as I don't like the bad feeling it gives me in my tummy. Mummy said I need to be careful about who I choose to be friends with. She always blames me when things go wrong. I was very happy when Chloe was my friend, but Mummy ruined it by telling me I was being too clingy. She hasn't got a clue what it's like for me. It's not my fault if Chloe started being nasty for no reason at all. Mummy invited her round for lunch last Saturday. Things were going really well until Katie stuck her big nose into things, so I kicked her. Chloe was *my* friend. Katie never shares her stuff, so why should I share Chloe? Chloe said she wanted to go home early and hasn't spoken to me since. Idiot!

Also, I hardly ever get invited to other people's houses and all the other mums in the playground give me funny looks. I don't know what their problem is.

Mummy has invited Ginny for tea...

## WHAT'S HAPPENING HERE?

There are many complex issues which complicate friendships for these children, whose closest relationships have been so hard.

Their developmental trauma makes them socially awkward, and their emotional development may also be delayed. Therefore they interact as if they were much younger, because they are working from their developmental age not their chronological age. Not having learned how to observe and then join in with a group, they will use younger methods to get attention, such as getting right in the child's face, copying them, or making up fabulous stories to fit in. If this does not work, they may pinch or push or even bite to get attention – toddler behaviour. This may earn them a reputation as being annoying or a bully. Such behaviours result in isolation and being cut off from the very groups they wish to engage with.

Abandonment issues get in the way. Charley is very vulnerable to the experience and expectation of rejection, as Peter left suddenly. On top of this, she has seen the fear-based behaviours of her older siblings, which is confusing for her.

If her new friend gets distracted or wants to play with someone else, the fear of being discarded prompts a disproportionate response, resulting in that child turning away from Charley.

Children can only learn from their own experiences. If they felt closest to their family and felt valued when they were bought a gift or fed, they will replicate this with gifts, money, sweets – anything to belong. But in the end, the other children pick up on their socially delayed behaviours or fall foul of their emotional developmental delay, and then the name-calling and exclusion commences. Sometimes, as here, the only friendships available are with the other 'odd ones out'; or the child may be lucky and find that rare empathic young person who will befriend them, but this is tiring for the friend and needs the careful management and support of their parents.

The drive for socialisation will be at odds with the child's issues of trust, so there will be hugely contrasting feelings to deal with. Traumatised children need help to discover how to say sorry, how to get over relationship bumps, and how to take care of friendships.

## ♟ REMEMBER...

✓ Our children cannot help the way they are. Their behaviours are trauma-based.

✓ They cannot learn difficult new ways of behaving without support.

✓ Meanwhile, they need help to achieve positive experiences.

## ♞ TRY THIS...

✓ Try to remind yourself that socialisation starts with family – try practising relationship skills, including making up after arguments (rupture and repair), at home before you apply them elsewhere.

✓ Support your child in a way that's appropriate to the age their behaviour shows you, not their chronological age.

✓ Help your child by having short, successful interactions.

✓ Reflect on why things have gone well (or badly) while the child is calm and responsive.

✓ Try to befriend the parents of other 'different' children. They will be more tolerant!

✓ Help your child by getting them involved in clubs or activities that they are skilled at, or specialist peer support that might be provided in your local area for children with a disability.

# 24

# Straight Talk, Please!

Within the care system, it is astonishing how language is used which is designed to protect feelings but ends up feeling patronising, and inaccurate. Some examples of this are given in this chapter and will be very familiar to many parents in similar situations.

It often seems that every aspect of the trauma experience and impact on the family is downplayed or re-imagined by using language which simply avoids the facts, or diminishes the parents or child.

These are real experiences...

✎ SARAH NAISH: Not 'just' a mum!

It's interesting how so many professionals seem to use language which appears designed to keep us all in the dark, and minimise us or the children!

Before I was 'William's Mum', I was Sarah, a social worker, a co-professional. Luckily, because of that, I understand some of the terminology used, but more and more I am finding it demeaning to us as a family, to the children and to me.

I have lost count of the number of therapists, social workers, teachers and other professionals who have called me 'Mum' or even worse 'Adoptive Mum' at meetings.

They wouldn't say, 'This is William, the autistic son.'

All the acronyms relating to social work and education are also unhelpful. Wouldn't it be easier if they just said what they meant?

Complete strangers think it's OK to ask about my children's private background.

It's not.

When I tell them this, they accuse me of being deliberately obstructive. Well, I am. Mind your nose. Or as my children would say, 'Trunky wanna bun?'

The following is some of the terminology I find the most offensive.

My FAMILY is not a CASE.

I am not a CARER. I am a PARENT. A skilled, knowledgeable, well-researched, *therapeutic* parent. I don't go off shift and go home!

If things went wrong, it wouldn't be a DISRUPTION – like a train arriving late or something – it would be a FAMILY BREAKDOWN.

When I go and see my parents, I don't have CONTACT with them. I VISIT them. Why can't we use the same language for our children?

As I am a single parent with five children, I was asked if I wanted 'RESPITE'. Well I do get my friend in sometimes so I can have a break, but respite? Seriously, what a horrendous term! I never thought about the impact of the word when I was working as a social worker.

The *most annoying* by far, however, is a term diminishing our relationship. My children are not PLACEMENTS. They are CHILDREN! And they are indeed my 'REAL' children.

## ଓ I AM NOT A PLACEMENT! (Any child, any age)

*I am NOT a placement. I'm a vulnerable, innocent child,*
*Not to be depersonalised, insulted and reviled.*
*I am NOT a nightmare, a burden or a brat.*
*I didn't ask to be here, so please don't call me that.*
*I am NOT a respite, short-term, long-term match.*
*I am a little person. A frightened one in fact!*
*I am NOT a solo. I'm the eldest child of three.*
*But due to my behaviours, they've granted enhanced fees.*
*I am NOT a LAC, a Step Down or a Bridge,*
*Chucked around the system like a secondhand fridge!*
*To live within a family should be my human right.*
*I should never have to ask,*
*'Where will I sleep tonight?'*

All I am is a placement. What does this mean? I wonder if they actually mean I'm a PLACEMAT? Placemats stay far longer in homes than I've ever done. I have lived with several families but am only just beginning to have one to call my own. Jackie and Kevin don't want me. They'd rather have the drugs.

I can't say that I blame them. No one wants me. I'm not surprised. I went away on respite recently; not sure what respite actually is, but it's got the word 'spite' in it, so it can't be that nice.

Another thing that really annoys me is when they call my brother and sisters 'siblings'. No one else at school calls their brothers and sisters 'siblings'. What planet are these people on? I just want to be like everyone else. These stupid words make me feel like a weirdo! I'm constantly reminded that I'm different, that I've been in care.

I used to have to attend stupid meetings called LAC reviews. Maybe I'm LACking something. I hate attending them and

I didn't go. I know another kid who has to sit with her old mum and not her foster mum.

I used to sit in a corner seat with my head down. But when I moved in with Sarah, she said I didn't have to go. Also, why do they call Sarah my carer? Carers look after people with dementia. I haven't got bloody dementia. I don't need a sodding carer. I'm not ill and it makes me feel like an outsider. I want to feel like I belong, I want to be a part of the family, not just a temporary addition. I know who gave birth to me, I'm not stupid. I just want to be a normal kid!

## WHAT'S HAPPENING HERE?

There is an information gap in the society in which we live. We see this most clearly when we look at the terminology used by supporting professionals, such as social workers, therapists and teachers. This is not a deliberate attempt to minimise the rights of the child or parent, nor is it an attempt to disregard their views. In fact, ironically, society has put into place all kinds of safeguards to 'hear the child' and 'respect the parent'.

The problem arises during training. The jargon which is used must be looked at closely, questioned and challenged. Why do we refer to families or children as 'cases'? This is not necessary. It creates division, ill-feeling and a sense of being diminished for the recipient of this terminology.

The child's view above clearly describes how they feel about the word 'respite'. 'Respite' is defined in the dictionary as 'a short period of rest or relief from something difficult or unpleasant'. Why on earth are we still using this term in the 21st century to describe the need for parents to have a break?

Traumatised children may often suffer the indignity of multiple questions, misinformation being shared about them, assumptions being made and never questioned, multiple tellings of their story, multiple promises, multiple disappointments, and a growing sense that no one is really interested.

## ☀ THINK...

- ✓ Think about the language you use every day.

- ✓ Are you talking about CHILDREN or PARENTS?

## ☙ TRY THIS...

- ✓ Replace discriminatory or upsetting words such as 'placement' and 'respite'. Think about the impact these words have on others.

- ✓ If these words or any others are used about you and your family and you find them offensive, tell the person who is using these words and explain why.

- ✓ If you drive your car, you are the driver. If you lend your car to someone else, the person driving it is still a driver. 'Parent', not 'carer' – always!

# 25

# **Dogs**

Pets are often already a big part of a family's life and it can be difficult integrating the conflicting needs of children, especially where safety needs to be considered too. However, dogs in particular can be very rewarding for both the parent and the child if early challenges can be overcome.

Before the children came home to live with Sarah, the social workers were worried about the children's fear of dogs, but dogs are a big part of her family's life. How have they all integrated? Is it positive or negative overall?

### SARAH NAISH: Pets and children

When the children came home to live with me I was aware that they were very frightened of dogs. I think there had been scary dogs in the birth family home. I was supposed to rehome my three small dogs, Albert, Sarnie and Cyril, but I didn't think it was a good idea to enable the children to go through life being scared of them. So I worked really hard to get them all comfortable with each other.

Well, that was a couple of years ago and, of course, Rosie and Katie are also part of the family now. Katie can be really controlling around the dogs and keeps picking them up and squeezing them just that little bit too tight! I watch them carefully though, and gradually things are improving. Today we were out for a walk and it was really scary because a big Irish wolfhound came along and attacked Albert. He is a very small Yorkshire terrier. The bigger dog literally picked him up and shook him like a rabbit. I was terrified but had to go against my instinct of running to grab him, so I could prevent the children from experiencing more trauma. I pushed them all quickly into a shelter so their view was blocked and told them to sit down. As I turned round, the owner had managed to free Albert and by some miracle he seemed OK. Normally, I would have been screaming too, I think. The children were beside themselves, especially Katie. We all sat together in the shelter and checked Albert over. I reassured the children he was OK but would have some bruises. They were so tender with him and seemed genuinely concerned for him, gently stroking him. As they did so, I noticed that not only was he calming down, but so were they.

Often, when Rosie loses her temper and starts screaming and shouting, I can point to Sarnie, who is shaking with fear, and say, 'Oh no, poor Sarnie. She looks terrified.' Amazingly, Rosie seems able to recognise this and she lowers her voice or walks away. Later, I always find her hugging Sarnie appropriately and appearing calm.

Sophie is obsessed with the dogs and always likes to have Cyril on her bed. They follow her around and she is very attentive and kind to them. This is the child who used to cry and try to climb up me to get away from them when she was 2 years old. The other day I asked her what she wanted to be when she grew up and she said, 'A Dalmatian!'

I am sure the dogs are calming the children and helping them to form real connections.

## I LOVE DOGS (Sophie, 9 years)

When I first came to live with Mummy, I was very scared of the dogs. I'm not sure why but I felt very worried that they might hurt me. I think something might have happened with dogs when I lived with Jackie and Kevin but I can't actually remember what it was. It was just a feeling in my chest. Mummy kept the dogs away from us at first, but I don't think it was for very long as we were soon running around with them. I can't remember when the scared feelings went away – it just sort of happened.

They made me feel calm when I stroked them and it helped to make the empty feeling in my tummy feel a bit fuller. Cyril is my favourite. I do love the others, but he knows when I'm feeling a bit wobbly, even when Mummy hasn't noticed. Recently, we were out with Mummy and a great big dog attacked Albert. He's very small and we were all very frightened. I thought that he was going to die! Mummy tried to keep us away from it all, but we could still hear everything and I thought my head was going to explode. The dogs are our family. What would we do if anything happened to Albert? Thankfully, he was OK although I think he was a bit sore. We gave him lots of cuddles and strokes and everybody felt a lot better.

It's really strange because even Rosie can calm down when she sees Sarnie shaking. Thank God someone can calm her down!

I love dogs sooo much that I often dream of sitting in the middle of a room full of dogs getting lots of hugs from them. I think that's why I always like to have Cyril on my bed with me. Dogs are so much easier to understand than people!

## WHAT'S HAPPENING HERE?

When Sarah first brings Sophie, William and Charley home, she instinctively knows that she can overcome their initial fearful reactions, and so she develops a strategy to help the children (and the dogs) get used to each other by using protected spaces.

Sarah notices how important the dogs have become in the household as a means for the children to give and receive unconditional love. Also, they have a calming – you could say a therapeutic – effect. Being around them, stroking them, taking responsibility for them appears to be relaxing. It seems to help bring Rosie's thinking brain back online if she can see that her actions are affecting Sarnie; and Sophie seems to find the comfort that she can receive from Cyril indispensable and she keeps him on her bed. Maybe he helps her feel safe and protected from the monsters.

The horrible attack perpetrated by the much bigger dog reveals another layer to the benefits of the dogs – the children seem to be relating to Albert empathically since the event, and stroking him and calming him down has a relaxing therapeutic effect on them as well.

Sophie's feelings about dogs are very clear – we see her move from fear to recognising their ability to make her feel better and to fill the empty feeling she has inside. They are able to do this because they are uncomplicated, loyal and loving. Sophie finds dogs are much easier to understand than people. Poor Sophie was very affected by the attack but she recognises that checking Albert over and stroking him made her feel better.

# ☲ REMEMBER...

✓ Pets have no hidden agenda.

✓ They respond quickly to loving affectionate care.

✓ It is well known how calming pets can be, with therapy dogs in schools, pets being taken to visit the elderly in homes, and even cat cafés where you can go and calm down with several cats happily purring or requesting attention nearby.

✓ Pets also teach us responsibility and the importance of caring for animals, as they cannot take care of themselves. This is an important lesson.

✓ The best thing about pets, however, is simply the way they can connect us so positively with our emotional self, and bring relief and healing.

# 26

# **Mess**

Many parents of traumatised children become exasperated at the amount of mess the children seem to cause. This is on a different scale to the usual untidiness associated with childhood.

In this chapter, Sarah establishes a strong routine and keeps everything in order. This is essential where children have had a chaotic start. But as the children grow and become more 'free range', the mess seems to spread!

✎ SARAH NAISH: Mess everywhere!

I actually cannot believe the amount of mess that one child can make! Well, of course, it's not actually one child – it's five children – but even so, I can see the individual messes created by each of them.

I think William and Sophie are the worst offenders – they just leave this trail of devastation in their wake and don't seem to realise what's happening. One of the social workers suggested they might have dyspraxia (a neurological condition which affects co-ordination and perception); but as we've got about 17 other diagnoses, I don't really take too much notice, to be honest. I did look up 'dyspraxia' and I can see it's also about not being able to be organised and having memory issues, but of course that applies to all the children.

When I go into their bedrooms – even if an hour ago I tidied everything up, made the beds, removed dirty washing, etc. – I can find that it looks like a small army of terrorists has marched through destroying everything in its path. I don't know how they do it. The mess is soul-destroying and so debilitating. It's a tsunami of mess. It never ends.

When I talk to people about this, they say ridiculous things like, 'Oh yes, all children make a mess.' This is in a different league! The rotting food in their schoolbags, the squalor in their rooms, the detritus that surrounds where they sit on the sofa and even all the debris in the space they occupy in the car! Little bits of chewed sweets taken out of their mouths and pressed into different patterns in the car seat are a daily occurrence.

The scenario is definitely like painting the 'Forth Road Bridge' (work on this massive bridge can never be completed, because as soon as they get to the end, the beginning needs repainting). I have realised that the house can never be tidy, so now I just limit myself to certain areas which I can keep habitable and then every Saturday we have a big purge on their bedrooms, just before pocket money time. This works OK, and the rest of the time I have to be strong and just shut the bedroom doors. If I just left them to it, I think the chaos in their rooms would resemble how it must've been when they lived with their birth family.

I thought they would appreciate everything being clean and structured – just another thing I got wrong!

## ⟲ WHAT MESS? (Sophie, 9 years)

I don't know why Mummy sometimes gets so cross about the mess in the house. It doesn't bother me at all. I'm far more comfortable in a messy room as I'm used to it. When I was tiny, I lived in a very messy and dirty home. No one seemed to care about it then. I remember eating old toast I found under the settee.

If I'm a bit upset, I feel much better after I rearrange everything, throw stuff on the floor, open the drawers and pull stuff out. It's like getting all the messy thoughts and feelings out of my head. It helps me to calm down. Once it's all untidy again, my scary feelings get a bit smaller and I can breathe more easily.

Sometimes I don't do it deliberately, it just sort of happens. One minute it's tidy and then William starts to play with me and everything is messy again.

When it's too tidy, I feel scared about making a mess in case I get into trouble.

Every Saturday we have a big tidy-up time and then we get our pocket money. I like getting pocket money as I can buy sweets. I don't mind tidying up on a Saturday, but Mummy often complains as I don't put things back in the right places. I honestly can't remember where stuff goes. I'm not sure Mummy believes me though.

William shoves everything underneath his bed, so it looks tidy when Mummy peeps her head around the door. Perhaps I should try doing the same.

We all get a bit wobbly in the car and Mummy gives us sweets to suck to help us feel better. William can't keep the sweet in his mouth and often rolls it all over the seat. It all gets very sticky. I quite like the feeling of touching the sticky places.

Mummy says the car is a right tip.

## WHAT'S HAPPENING HERE?

We are human. We seek familiarity – we are attracted to people who look like us, who like the same things, have the same interests.

These children have survived trauma so have a strong link with their past and the things that felt familiar and strangely safe.

There are other factors too: maybe mess gives you a place to hide where you will not be noticed. Maybe the old food has been stashed during a moment of anxiety – it's easy to forget you get fed when you were starving for so long.

Mum is right: the chaos and confusion recreates the birth home. The thing is, in that home they knew how to be, how to act, how to survive. When it all gets too much, it's easier to go back to that place, to recreate it. Then they know how to manage. And the sweets on the car seat? Well, maybe when you have suffered sensory deprivation for two years after birth, you learn to get the most out of every sensory experience. A sweet activates your sense of taste but it's also a ball that you can roll around (a little dirt and lint never stopped you eating anything – you didn't always have a choice!) and then you can enjoy that sticky feeling.

## ♟ REMEMBER...

- ✓ Our children are trying to cope in a world that is completely alien to them. Some children will manage better than others because of the individual nature of experiences and resilience, but all this is hard for them. Their universe has shifted, nothing is the same. They are safe, but it does not feel safe at all.

- ✓ Children will not be able to trust their new experiences until they have had these reinforced many hundreds of times.

# ☙ TRY THIS...

✓ Moving too fast will cause overwhelm, and being cross will drive them into shame, so use empathy and be patient.

✓ Try to understand their experience.

✓ Allow them their space but have a rule to keep *your* spaces clear; then close the bedroom door.

✓ Try to keep in mind that children sometimes externalise their inner distress by creating chaos and mess. Ironically, while this may cause you stress, it can help regulate your child.

# 27

# **Blame**

Looking after traumatised children presents a myriad of complex problems to solve. When these problems seem overwhelming, it is easy to slip back into a position of blame. Blame is easier to do than trying to solve the issues surrounding challenging behaviours.

There seems to be a lot of blame flying about in this chapter. Sarah experiences it differently to the children though.

### ✎ SARAH NAISH: Blame game

Feeling blamed. Feeling judged. All the time – by professionals, friends, well-meaning family members. It's worse when it's the social workers. Whatever happens, they offer fake sympathy, but always imply that my parenting is at fault. Probably I don't set boundaries. Probably I am the one who is too anxious. Probably I am exaggerating. Anyone can see that my child is fine; really, it's me that is the problem. I worry too much, talk too much, talk too little. Clearly, I do not offer consequences, I just give in. I probably never talk to my child about their feelings. As if! Sometimes I do get some back-up, like the time the child and adolescent mental health nurse spoke on my behalf, but this was discounted by the social workers, who clearly know better.

The worst thing is that the person who blames and judges me most is me. My children can't help themselves. I should be able to do better, do more – and gradually I sink back into my black hole, under my stone, and hide away from the world again.

Even after all these years, I find that I still get triggered; I still get the snakes in my stomach and a grip around my heart. When does it end?

## ✎ SARAH NAISH: The unintentional warrior

Our children were not born into peace and tranquillity. They were born needing to protect themselves, to learn fast, to adapt to the difficulties they face.

They did not choose this life. They have had to become warriors. They have had to learn to fight for things which others just take for granted. When they fight, we say they are controlling or defiant.

They didn't want to be warriors. They wanted to be children.

When our children come to live with us, we have to start sorting it out. We wanted a family, a normal loving family, but we have to realign ourselves with therapeutic parenting. We have to explain why we parent the way we do. We have to roar at schools and the system which tries to break our children.

We didn't want to be warriors. We wanted to be parents.

We are all unintentional warriors. But at least we are walking the same way and fighting the same war.

## ❦ I DON'T WANT TO FIGHT (Rosie, 10 years)

I don't want to have to fight, but what choice do I have? I've never known anything else. I get blamed for everything. Absolutely everything! School is a nightmare for me. The teachers think I'm bad, naughty, rude. I suppose they're right but I didn't ask to be this way. I didn't choose to be bad, rotten to the core, disruptive, aggressive and defiant. I've heard it all... It's no wonder my birth parents treated me so badly. I remember waking up terrified of what was to come. Would we be fed, would we be hurt, would the curtains ever be opened? I had to learn how to fight, hide, steal food, lie, protect my brother and sisters. How else was I to survive?

Sarah says I can trust her, but I'm scared. I've never trusted adults. How can I? I can't even call her 'Mum'. It makes me feel physically sick. 'Sarah' is much safer. I don't know why.

I got into BIG TROUBLE recently after locking a teacher in a cupboard. What did she expect after she insisted I draw my feelings! I couldn't breathe properly. I thought I might die. I feel so sad and angry inside and I know it comes out at the wrong times and with the wrong people. Sarah tells me to try to be good. I do try. I try every single day but it doesn't work. Adults always think they're right and sometimes I think of ways I can 'get them back'.

I remember telling the dinner ladies that Sarah hadn't given me any breakfast. Mrs Taylor gave me extra chips. Sarah was very cross after a meeting with the Headteacher at the end of the day.

## WHAT'S HAPPENING HERE?

It is interesting. Everyone is so worried about who will be found to be at fault that the blame starts flying around. Rosie blames herself: everything must have been her fault. She must have been a very bad baby indeed or Jackie and Kevin would have loved her and cared for her properly. Anything bad that happened to the chilldren *must* be their fault, mustn't it? That's what they were told.

Professionals look at behaviours. They see that the worst behaviours often occur at home and around parents, and then feel they have identified the cause, forgetting that these children have a huge burden of mistrust and fear which drives anxious, controlling, fearful, angry behaviours. The feelings of trust and comfort children experience only make them feel more vulnerable, and cause them to lash out and reject.

Schools, not understanding that patterns of dysregulation (extreme and uncontrolled behaviours) at home are actually a sign of security, feel that the home environment is at fault. The child is no problem at school; or if they are a problem at school, then they are clearly unmanageable, or need to see that they have to do as they are told, and be subject to the same punishments as other children if they fidget, fail to concentrate or display controlling behaviours.

When parents are fully able to describe the issues for themselves, they find that what they say is diminished – for example, they might report a violent attack (the latest of many such incidents) due to massive overwhelm in the face of unknown stressors, and find themselves faced with a social worker saying that they understand things are 'a little bit tricky' at present; then maybe a solution is offered: going on a parenting course or using a reward chart?!!

Parents tell us that they are often treated as though they have no real input or insight into the behaviours that they are dealing with 24/7. They report being excluded from meetings for 'professionals' because they are only 'parents'. The fact is, therapeutic parents become experts in a very specialised field – their children.

## ♀ REMEMBER...

✓ Blame and judgement do nothing to improve the situation. We need to offer individual solutions to individual families. *We need to support, not blame.* We need to offer strategies, and remember that these will take time. We also need to have appropriate expectations and above all empathy for our struggling parents, and for the children whose life lessons have been so hard that for some it takes many years to recover and find ways of dealing with the world.

✓ We need to take care of those who are looking after our most vulnerable and disenfranchised children. We need to help them stay away from blame and judgement, and to give them faith in their abilities and commitment; otherwise they may fall into despair and become the next parents to give up.

✓ See also Chapter 10, 'When Things Get Stuck', and Chapter 36, 'School'.

# 28

# **Diagnoses**

Parents often struggle to get the correct diagnosis for their child. How do parents know that it is the right one? Often a parent will feel that there is something more seriously wrong, but this has been minimised. On top of this, sometimes it can be a very long wait to see the right consultant.

This family, like many others, is subjected to a plethora of diagnoses which are trying to make sense of the difficulties the children have. This does not seem to be making life any easier!

A list at the back of the book explains some of the conditions mentioned in this chapter.

### ✎ SARAH NAISH: Confused

My head is spinning and I just cannot work it out any more.

So far, between them, the children have a variety of diagnoses including dyspraxia (linked with memory, organisation, motor skills and co-ordination issues due to clumsiness), sensory processing disorder (SPD), attachment disorder, autism spectrum disorders (ASD) including Asperger's, global developmental delay, epilepsy, attention deficit hyperactivity disorder (ADHD), and attention deficit disorder. Teachers have also mentioned oppositional defiant disorder (ODD).

I am sorry, but I just don't buy it anymore.

If Rosie has epilepsy, how come none of the symptoms fit properly? How come the medication makes it worse? How come it's stress-related? It does not fit.

If she has attention deficit disorder, how come she only needs medication for this at school and we don't have these issues at home? We seem to manage the symptoms through strong routine and boundaries.

It cannot be the case that spending years in a family where there was daily abuse and fear had no impact...of course it can't. My instinct is that these diagnoses are a way for the medical profession to try to compartmentalise the varying symptoms of a much more serious underlying condition.

Of course, the children have attachment difficulties – that is as plain as the nose on my face. They did not learn to form relationships and did not learn that adults were safe, so we are starting at the bottom rung there.

The diagnoses they do have help us a bit at school. Teachers know that sensory processing disorder means they have to be sensitive about sudden noises and lights, etc. They also understand about the need for routine.

The reason I think lots of different diagnoses are in-appropriate and incorrect is because the children show huge improvements in some areas. For example, my niece Charlotte is the same age as William and has dyspraxia. Her condition has remained the same and she continues to need the same levels of help with organisation. She is very unsteady and falls easily. William used to be like this and that's why he had the same diagnosis, but nowadays he is nowhere near as bad as he used to be. His balance is better and he is more organised, although he still needs support. They said he was autistic as he was so closed down and had problems communicating, but those issues have diminished significantly. You don't 'grow out' of dyspraxia and autism.

Something else is going on here, but it's so frustrating trying to find therapists and doctors who have the remotest clue! They just want to pigeonhole the children.

## WHAT IS WRONG WITH ME? (All children)

*They don't know what's wrong with me.*
*Some say I have ADHD.*
*Others say it's attachment related.*
*Their manual needs to be updated!*

*My problems stem from all my trauma.*
*Unmet needs have caused disorder.*
*My front brain hasn't come online.*
*I'm stuck in survival all the time.*

*My teacher said it's ODD.*
*I can't allow control of me.*
*I'm oppositional and defiant.*
*As I'm used to being self-reliant.*

*Perhaps I have PDA.*[1]
*That's why I push them all away.*
*After that I reel them in.*
*It's the only way that I can win.*

*Maybe I have an ASD.*
*I've not learned to do empathy,*
*I line my stuff up in a row,*
*Trying to get my brain to grow.*

*The GP thinks it's SPD.*
*A referral to the new OT.*[2]

---

1  PDA stands for Pathological Demand Avoidance. It is characterised by obsessively resisting ordinary demands, appearing sociable but lacking depth in understanding, excessive mood swings and obsessive behaviours.
2  Occupational therapist.

*It's now official, she has said,*
*A weighted blanket[3] for my bed.*

*Lots of labels on my file,*
*An EHCP[4] for quite a while,*
*An urgent request for therapy,*
*Will CAMHS[5] have the space for me?*

*My personality is on the border.[6]*
*I've now got a new disorder.*
*Taking meds late at night.*
*So I can sleep without a fight.*

*I only wish that they could see*
*What is truly wrong with me.*
*It's all developmental trauma,*
*The rest are symptoms of the disorder.*

## FREAK (William, 8 years)

I feel like a freak at times. I've been to see loads of doctors, therapists, etc. They have given me lots of different lists of what's wrong with me. If I didn't feel like a failure before, I do now. No wonder Jackie and Kevin didn't think I was worth looking after.

Apparently, I have about 13 disorders and autistic traits on top. Mummy won't be able to cope with me. I feel like faulty goods. I'm bad, disgusting and not good enough.

I just want to know what is WRONG with me!

---

3   A weighted blanket is used for children especially with sensory processing disorder who find it comfortable to be swaddled and held and enjoy the feeling of weight to reinforce this.
4   Education, Health and Care Plan.
5   Child and Adolescent Mental Health Services.
6   Borderline personality disorder is a disorder affecting mood and ability to manage relationships. Symptoms include emotional instability, confused perceptions, impulsive behaviour, intense but unstable relationships.

## WHAT'S HAPPENING HERE?

Like so many parents, Sarah is looking for reasons and underlying conditions, or at least for some help and advice! But the answers bring up more questions. It simply does not add up. The list of diagnoses grows, but the medicines do not seem to be effective. It seems like what *is* getting a positive response is the therapeutic parenting strategies that Sarah is using to counter the symptoms. How very strange that this huge range of symptoms and behavioural disorders all seem to be responsive to appropriate parenting techniques!

The child – a composite child here – is able to look at all of these diagnoses and suggest an alternative. Perhaps what is happening is that every child is showing individual responses to the same issue – developmental trauma – partly as a result of the chemical interactions in their body and their birth mum's, and partly as a result of their experiences of neglect and abuse, which differ from child to child and therefore emerge differently in each case. This is compounded by the lack of an attuned adult to help them to build a strong and confident internal working model, and to demonstrate to these children how beautiful they are.

## ♟ REMEMBER...

- ✓ Using therapeutic parenting techniques enables any child to engage with the world in an entirely different way. New neuronal connections are made, enabling development of areas of the brain that need to be activated and stimulated for the child to fill their developmental gaps, overcome their obstacles and become the best people that they can be.

- ✓ This is not just about cognitive ability, but about social, emotional and physical capability as well. Throughout the book we have described these interactions and the benefits that result.

## ⚙ THINK...

✓ Diagnoses can have one really good result, which is to provide evidence to enable schools to get additional funding for support and education. Additionally parents may be able to use diagnoses to access support groups and discover new strategies. In the UK the SEND (special educational needs and disability) system supports a child's needs when supported by evidence up to the age of 25.

# 29

# **Sabotage**

One of the hardest issues that parents face is when their child is unable to accept the nicer things in life. Sometimes it feels like the harder the parents work to make a special day or gift, the harder the child works to spoil it in some way.

It can feel like sabotage. In this chapter, Sarah feels as if the children deliberately ruin the day and everyone else's. But maybe we need to take a closer look...

✎ SARAH NAISH: The trip to the zoo

So, yet another nice day out ruined! I don't know why I bother. It's so dispiriting.

The plan was to go to the zoo and take a lovely picnic lunch. I told all the children this morning what we were going to do and they all seemed pleased and excited.

First of all, we had the whole 'let's go out in ripped and dirty clothing' nonsense to get over. This took all my patience and negotiating skills! I should have set their clothes out the night before.

On the way there (amazingly), there was only one incident in the car where Rosie and Katie had a shouting argument, complete with slapping and other behaviours requiring a referee.

Once we got to the zoo there was so much silly behaviour it was unbelievable. William did not want to look at any of the animals because they 'were staring at him'. Rosie walked around all day with a face like thunder and her arms folded. She managed to force herself to have lunch but was very unhappy it was a picnic rather than a meal in the café. She was very vocal about the failings of the picnic, which I had spent over an hour preparing.

Sophie and Charley both managed to poo themselves at the same time, which was fun trying to sort out in the public toilets with all the parents judging me. Once I had sorted them out, I noticed William had wet himself but appeared oblivious. I seem to spend a lot of time in public loos!

On the way home, it was a complete nightmare: a full-on punch-up in the back of the car, with another screaming contest and William being sick, literally everywhere. Rosie said the zoo idea was really stupid and she isn't going on any other 'days out for losers'.

They are *so* ungrateful! Nothing I ever do is enough and they don't appreciate anything. It's ruined, thrown back in my face or discarded somehow.

I don't think I can be bothered anymore, but life will be *so* boring!

The more I plan for a nice time, the more I pay.

## THE REAL CHILD (Rosie, 11 years)

Sarah said I keep spoiling things, ruining all the nice things we do together.

Of course I do. Is she an idiot or what?

I ruin everything because I don't feel right when I do nice things and sometimes I feel like she's trying to set me up! If we do good stuff together and then she gets angry later, she might tell me I'm not grateful.

She's said this before and it makes me really angry. I don't feel bloody grateful!

What if she's trying to trick me and wants something back in return?

Also, it means she thinks she's getting close to me and that is just too scary.

I heard her on the phone to her friend the other day saying she thinks she's turning a corner with me as sometimes I laugh. What does this mean? Turning what corner?

After the visit to the zoo, I felt sick. I felt a bit happy and I don't like being happy because then it's worse again when the sadness comes back.

I'm not a nice person on the inside, so I shouldn't have laughed so much. Oh, and I nearly forgot: when we had to leave the zoo, I felt really sad… I mean really, really sad. Sometimes it's easier not to enjoy yourself, then you won't feel sad when it ends. I'm so stupid.

## WHAT'S HAPPENING HERE?

Sarah feels like she is banging her head against a brick wall. My goodness, she is trying so hard to give the children lovely experiences and make up the time that they have lost. She wants to at least fill some of the gaps in their experience, and her sadness at what she perceives as her failure is tangible. Also, what *is* she supposed to do to help them? It seems like even simple activities are too much for them to cope with.

The children, meanwhile, are scared rigid. Everything about the day seems to be overwhelming and scary, to the point where they are literally sick and voiding their bowels. The animals are staring at them; they feel very dangerous.

There are lots of strangers there. Who knows what they will do? Our voice of the child explains what is happening for her: it feels wrong to have nice things – she has not had experience of this. She knows she does not deserve nice experiences. She knows she is not nice. She does not deserve anything other than harsh and cruel treatment, because she is so bad. She has always been bad – ever since she was born. So nice experiences literally make her feel uncomfortable, and actually, the only time nice events were planned in the past was because there would be a pay-back later. What will Mum make her do? And with whom? And always, inevitably, there is an end to all the niceness, and it feels like the end of everything nice, forever.

## ♟ REMEMBER...

- ✓ The ability of our children to feel that they are bad is linked to their internal working model, which has formed an idea of self, based on their experience.

- ✓ Having no frame of reference that does not involve abuse, neglect, pain and the ways in which adults can misuse you because they are in total control of you, ensures that your core concept is that you are very bad.

- ✓ This leads to pervasive shame. The basic developmental tasks that allow us to separate our actions from ourselves have not happened.

## ⚑ TRY THIS...

- ✓ Keep the early experience of the child in mind. When we first introduce a baby to the world, we are careful to keep their interactions short and sweet and to give them time to process. We understand when things get a bit much and take them to a quiet place to calm down.

✓ To help your child engage in ordinary activities, you need to replicate this early behaviour, giving a child brief glimpses of happy experiences and then allowing them to process.

✓ To begin with, these experiences will revolve around connecting to us, so walks in the park or time spent doing ordinary domestic things together will help to build a safer feeling.

✓ Only once a more or less secure relationship is established will the child be able to manage the bigger events.

✓ Let's not set them up to fail. This might mean dipping in and out of family days, or not going at all until the child is more secure.

✓ Stop and think about the sensory nature of big adventure days. Maybe a low-key approach will be more relaxing for you all – and much less expensive!!

## ♟ REMEMBER...

✓ As adults looking after such vulnerable young people, we have to remember that being grateful is not something that they have learned. Or it may be that they were punished for not being 'grateful' for the insufficient care that they received.

✓ They need to be supported to say 'thank you' and to manage inevitable disappointment like any young child who is new to the experience.

# 30

# What Lies Beneath (the Internal Working Model)

It can be extremely difficult for children who have been abused or neglected, and left in fear in some way in their early life, to have any sense that they are worth loving. There is a constant conflict with what they need and what they are able to accept.

The children's early relationships with adults will have informed the way that they feel about themselves – their emerging sense of self – and also about new adults they encounter, and everything else in the world.

Look what happens when initial experiences which brought pain and fear collide with the new 'script' which Sarah is providing... and keeps reinforcing.

✎ SARAH NAISH: A good heart

I understand that Rosie feels the need to convince me she is a 'bad person'. She rejects me and sabotages anything positive.

But I see these glimpses of the 'real Rosie'. As the trauma issues start to diminish slightly, I see the real child. I want to tell her that she *is* worth it. That she *is* a good person, but I know she can't hear me or accept my view. I want to tell her this:

I see your good heart, beating strongly.

I hear your denials and anger to prove me wrong again.

I see the confusion on your face when I give you praise. It breaks my heart.

I found the scribbled-over drawing that I accidentally said was great.

I give you what little I can to help you know you *are* worth it, but this is thrown back at me, destroyed, damaged, rejected scornfully.

I see your little kindnesses, I see through your propaganda, but you don't.

You don't see your good heart, your potential, your humour, your cleverness, the way you never give up, your strength.

And nothing I can say seems to make you see what I see. The child beneath. My little warrior. My hero. My inspiration.


## MY BLACK HEART (Rosie, 11 years)

I don't know why she says I'm a good person. Why does she keep lying to me like this?

I know I'm not good, if I was, Jackie wouldn't have let us get hurt! She would have protected us and made sure we were fed properly. I can't see why she didn't do what mums are supposed to do. The only thing I can think of is that I was a disappointment in some way. Perhaps I'm unlovable. I know I'm bad. My heart is black, full of wickedness and failure.

When Sarah tells me I've made a good job of something, it makes me so angry. I get a big whooshy feeling of hate rise up into my chest. It travels down my arms and I end up ripping up stuff or stomping off, waving my arms frantically.

I know this makes her sad. I always end up making people sad. I really must be bad.

I do want to be nice, honestly I do. Sometimes I call Sarah 'Mummy' and I get a warm feeling in my tummy, but it quickly turns back to scared feelings. If I let her get too close and she finds out what I'm really like...

I can't bear to lose another person, so it's best I don't get close to anyone.

I make sure she doesn't forget how bad I am, and so I remind her regularly of my evil 'black heart'.

## WHAT'S HAPPENING HERE?

In this case, Sarah already understands the issues. However, there is a disconnect in the way Rosie views herself and the way Mum sees her true potential. Rosie is beginning to trust Sarah, so we see the start of her experimenting with using 'Mummy' instead of Sarah.

### Parent's internal working model (IWM)

Based on a 'good enough' experience where needs are consistently met, and ruptures to relationships are repaired, a parent may have the following IWM of a family:

- *Adults:* Safe, loving, reliable, trustworthy, resilient, stable, responsible.

- *Children:* represent love, fun, exploration, family playtime and nurture. Parents can educate and protect their children and grow as a family.

- *World:* the world is safe and wonderful so the family can happily explore and have fun-filled new experiences.

### Child's internal working model (IWM)

The child's experiences will have developed their internal working model of their understanding of themselves, adults and the world. Being moved into care necessarily means that there has been trauma in the life of this child, giving rise to a child for whom family has a different meaning:

- *Self*: Bad, unlovable, worthless, no good, rubbish, ashamed, fearful, hurting, invisible, horrible, stupid.

- *Adults*: Unsafe, cruel, cause pain, terrifying, unreliable, untrustworthy, inconsistent, negligent, violent.

- *World*: Unsafe, terrifying, need to fight to survive, hostile. New experiences are overwhelming.

## 🏆 REMEMBER...

- ✓ It is clear that these two experiences cannot match. What sometimes happens is that the child seems to adapt really well but then cannot contain their fears and anxieties any longer. For them the loving experiences are unnatural, unsafe and uncomfortable. This is terrible for the parents, who feel their own sense of chaos, failure, shame and a world spiralling out of control. This can lead to compassion fatigue, family breakdown and further heartbreak all round.

## 🔑 TRY THIS...

- ✓ *Consistency*, *predictability* and *reliability* build brains. Rewiring a child's brain takes baby steps, time, patience, routine, boundaries and love.

✓ Low-level consistent positive reinforcement is much easier for the child to integrate into their internal working model, so avoid over-praising, which can create a conflict for them.

# 31

# **Memory**

Trauma can have a devastating impact on a child's memory. They struggle to retain information which is needed for day-to-day activities. For the parents, this can be confusing and irritating. Sometimes it is hard to believe that the children are not doing it on purpose!

Sarah writes in this chapter about seeing first-hand the impact of trauma on the children's memory and tries to unpick the resulting effects.

✎ SARAH NAISH: The memory carousel

I've always known that my children struggle to remember things. Over the last few months it's become more and more apparent that there are big holes in their memory. I'm not talking about distant memory and how they struggle to remember negative things that happened to them in the past. I think it's understandable that our brains protect us from some of the dreadful things that happened.

I mean the times when we go on a day out and the next day some of the children have no recollection of that.

I think of it as 'the memory carousel'. It just feels like, periodically, different memories from say three or four weeks ago flit back into the children's minds and they remember the event. Sometimes though, it might be a lot longer than that – maybe three or six months.

Today Rosie came home from school saying she had to do a project on Paris. I was really pleased because we only went there three weeks ago. She said she had never been and I must have taken the others without her. I showed her the videos and she seemed really confused. I truly think that she is convinced that I did some kind of magic and Photoshopped her into the video!

I hope the children will one day have a sense of memory of all the things that we do. But I do ask myself, if they can't even remember the lovely things we do how on earth are they supposed to remember school work and perform well in tests? It is ludicrous nonsense.

On top of these longer-term memory problems, I've noticed that they don't retain essential information for everyday tasks. Either that or they are being lazy! It doesn't matter how many times I remind them about PE kits, lunch boxes, etc., they look at me like it's the first time they ever heard it. I have lost count of the number of times I get them to school and then find an essential piece of equipment back in the car or at home.

Everything gets forgotten. School just thinks I am the most disorganised mum they have ever met!

## &#x24E0; PARIS (Rosie, 12 years)

A very strange thing happened today. We are doing a stupid project at school about Paris.

I think my teacher said it's a place in France. We looked at lots of pictures and it was a bit interesting. Only a bit though.

I spent ages looking at a picture of the Eiffel Tower. It seemed strangely familiar, but I don't have a clue why.

We watched a little film and it looked like a very busy place. There were lots and lots of restaurants though, so maybe it is a nice place.

When I got home this evening, I told Mummy Sarah about the project.

Unfortunately, she looked a bit excited, so I told her it was very boring.

Mummy Sarah then told me that I have been to Paris and it wasn't that long ago.

I thought that was a big fat lie. How could that be possible? Surely I would have remembered.

I felt a big feeling in my chest, my head felt strange. Mummy Sarah said I must have been confused and showed me pictures of myself in Paris. And a VIDEO of me stood outside the Eiffel Tower!

How could this be?

I don't understand. Mummy Sarah thinks I may have forgotten. I think I have a bit of a problem remembering things. But it's not my fault! Everyone else is stupid telling me too much stuff!

I got told off last week for forgetting my PE kit. I didn't know we have PE on Tuesdays. The teacher said we always have PE on a Tuesday. All the other children were looking at me with their mouths open and the teacher was shaking her silly head yet again. I felt embarrassed and that made me very cross. It feels like I've got a hole in my brain and lots of memories fall into it. Sometimes they pop back out and it's a bit of a surprise.

Granny says it's very interesting how I never forget where the biscuit tin is. Strangely enough, I always remember where the nice food is kept.

It's very scary to forget things. Very scary indeed.

## WHAT'S HAPPENING HERE?

A change is happening in the way Rosie is thinking about Sarah. She has moved from 'Sarah' to thinking about her as 'Mummy', and now 'Mummy Sarah'. This is a significant shift.

With memory functioning there are three functions at work here:

1. The way that we create and store a memory based on feeling states.

2. Our sensory input (what we see, hear, smell, taste and feel during an experience).

3. The capacity of our brain to process, manage and learn – executive function.

The trip to Paris is intended as a lovely trip for the family, but for Rosie, it is a potentially terrifying experience. Her brain, hardwired to protect and survive, is in an intensely stressful situation – so her focus will have been on possible threats and safety due to her hypervigilance which directly relates to her trauma.

The sights and scenes pass her by in favour of managing the trip, not being left behind, and keeping her siblings safe – and this is unconscious. It is as though her sensory input is shut down to enable focus on the threat. This is a survival response. She will then not have a clear explicit memory of the event.

### Brain function

Where there is neglect and abuse, there is likely to be a lack of development in the brain of the *frontal lobe* – the part of the brain associated with impulse control and organisation. There will also be an associated lack of development in the *hippocampus* – the part of the brain associated with memory. Therefore, the child will have tremendous difficulty in transferring short-term memory into long-term memory. As a result, the child will live in an almost 'Groundhog Day' situation and will struggle to differentiate between past and present.

### Executive function

Organisation and planning are part of the executive function of the brain. This is activated by the consistent, predictable and reliable routines and expectations we form as part of our earliest experiences. These routines give us a 'pattern' – a template – and allow us to understand cause and effect and consequences and to control impulsivity. However, where there has been chaos, neglect and abuse, these concepts are unclear – there is no predictability, no pattern. What happens today or even this minute is immaterial. Things change minute to minute.

### Working memory

Working memory, a common component in developmental trauma, is a function of short-term memory which can be massively compromised by trauma, making retention of information extremely hard.

## ℞ TRY THIS...

- ✓ Be the child's executive function – support, remind, organise.

- ✓ Use visual aids – timetables, photos, checklists.

- ✓ Give only one instruction at a time.

- ✓ Have photos or photo books of trips, etc. to remind them. Talk about those experiences – use past experiences to help them manage new experiences.

✓ Remember that they will learn in time with support. As part of their development they need this support as though they were tiny.

✓ Make school aware of the impact of their memory problems, especially in relation to tests, etc!

# 32

# **Contact**

Occasions when children are taken to see members of their birth family can often act as a flashpoint, creating tension and awakening hidden trauma. Sometimes the relationships are positive. Often they are not.

Parents might dread the build-up to these occasions, and it's even harder when the contact has been ordered and all those who know the child can see it is doing more harm than good.

In this chapter Sarah and Rosie are thinking about the very difficult issues and worries, mainly historical in this particular scenario, when there are visits or 'contact' with the birth family.

### ✏ SARAH NAISH: Horror visits

I was speaking to another adopter at a coffee morning today. She was telling me how she has to take her children to 'contact' once a year. She described how there is this horrendous build-up to the day, where the children act up and all their behaviour deteriorates. I can't imagine going through that. I think we were lucky. In the early days, Social Services arranged contact between the children and their birth family at a family centre. This was stopped when Kevin threatened to kill one of the children during a supervised visit.

If they ever tried to restart it, I can honestly say that I would put all the children in the car and drive away. How could I help the children to feel safe if I took them to see the people who abused them? The very thought makes my blood run cold.

I know not all birth parents are like that. When I worked as a social worker, I helped a birth mum keep up some really positive visits with her little boy. She did genuinely love him but she had learning difficulties and could not keep any kind of routine together.

When I fostered, the birth mum visited every day at our house. It was really dreadful for everyone. The mum tried hard but every time she came the children were torn between staying safe with me or returning to a father who abused them. The birth father never came, but I know that he knew where we lived. I was always scared he would turn up. He was a very violent man.

With my children, even now, I have to show William that I have locked the doors every night. His nightmares are about Kevin getting in the house or finding him somehow.

The therapist told us to remove the pictures of the birth parents from the children's life story books as it was re-traumatising them. Turns out she was right about that at least. The children settled better at night once those pictures were gone.

So, if that's how traumatic just the pictures were, I can't imagine what an actual visit would be like. That's why I would leave with the children and never come back.

## NO ONE ASKED US (Rosie, 12 years)

I overheard a conversation between Mummy and another mum today. We were at a coffee morning at the soft play. I was meant to be at school but I said I had a tummy ache. I didn't though.

I don't think Mummy believed me, but she said we could have some 'mum and daughter time' Yuck!

Mummy said I could go with her to the coffee morning. I was pretending to play with another child but I don't miss a thing! Mummy says I've got bat ears.

The other mum was talking about her children. She said they still had to see their old parents, the ones who hurt them!

I'm so happy that I don't have to see Jackie and Kevin anymore. My mummy said that will *never* happen. But thinking about it made me really wobbly and then I *did* get a tummy ache. It made me think of the times when we did have to go.

We had to go to this huge building with the social worker. There was a big gap thing on the wall. The social worker said the kitchen was behind it, and I could hear banging. I couldn't concentrate because of the banging noises. Even now, I don't like those at school. Apparently, they are called 'serving hatches'.

When we were with different foster parents, Katie and I used to meet William, Sophie and Charley at the centre. Then Jackie and Kevin would come in. I had to pretend everything was fine. When he held Charley, it made me feel sick. They made me feel sick. No one cared that we were scared. Katie always wet herself.

I used to just try to behave the same way I used to. I did get lots of sweets usually but it was weird because I didn't really want them. I didn't want anything from them. I didn't want to touch anything they touched.

Sophie didn't remember as much and she always took the sweets and smiled at them. I could see her teeth though. It wasn't like how she smiles now. It was a scared face smile.

I had no choice. The adults decided everything. The social workers used to have a nice chat and coffee. Kevin was always making secret signals at me. Telling me to keep my mouth shut.

I didn't tell Mummy the truth about him for three years. I had to make sure he wasn't coming back. I couldn't escape. I was trapped, scared, frozen. Why did they do that? My foster mum said she'd keep me safe. Well that was a lie! She TOOK me there!

No one asked us. No one listened, No one cared... But if they had asked us what we wanted, I couldn't have told the truth anyway! Kevin might have killed me for that.

The social workers told us they weren't safe... Like I didn't know! Then made us stay in a room with them. It made no sense.

I am so glad we don't have to see them ever again. Mummy promised and she does keep promises. I've checked.

## WHAT'S HAPPENING HERE?

Visiting with birth parents or other family members – contact – is not simple.

'Contact' is deemed to be important to enable children to retain their history and to help them with their construction of their identity. For some parents and children this can work, and there is an example given above. But for some children these visits are literally a horrific experience where they are exposed to threats from their parents. There are also cases where further abuse has occurred during these times.

Children are left feeling very unsafe – how can they believe promises made by social workers and their new families if they are brought face to face with those who abused them in the first place?

Looking at Rosie's story, we can see that coming face to face with her parents brought back terrible memories and fears. Kevin was able to threaten her to keep silent, and she knew what would happen if she failed in this. Kevin had been all-powerful, and in that household, children had died. We give children mixed messages:

we remove them because they are not safe, then we tell them they are having a visit with Mummy and Daddy. Won't that be nice?

The child is not able to make sense of these conflicts, which only adds to their own fear that somehow they are responsible.

## ♟ REMEMBER...

- ✓ There is no 'one size fits all' when it comes to families. Ideally, we would take each child according to their own circumstances and make a separate appropriate choice, for foster families as well as for adoption, kinship carers or special guardians.

- ✓ For some this will mean visits (if there is a chance of rehabilitation) so that the parent can develop skills.

- ✓ For others, there may be extended members of the family who are safe to have contact with.

- ✓ Brothers and sisters can remain connected, and this (although triggering) may ultimately be part of how they come to understand their story; but, again, it depends on circumstances. If a child has been raped by their sibling, they should not be made to endure a meeting. For some, maybe letters could be a way to keep in touch.

- ✓ Whatever their story, it is really important to hear the child. Hearing the child is not just about asking them a question, it is about observing them and the impact of the visit and taking their overall experience into account.

- ✓ Some children wish for contact. Some cannot manage. Some may seek parents later, as adults. Whatever the circumstances, the child's needs should be paramount, not the rights of the parent.

# 33

# Lying

One of the main behaviours which parents of traumatised children find exasperating is lying. It seems quite illogical. The children lie as if their life depends on it, perhaps because they feel like it does. Faced with this frustrating situation, many times a day, patience can wear very thin.

Lying seems to be a real issue for Sarah and the children. Even as they are growing older, this remains a problem. Nothing is more annoying than trying to deal with someone telling you a bare-faced lie and expecting you to believe it!

## ✎ SARAH NAISH: Liar

I was really shocked when I realised that the only time my children look me straight in the eye is when they are lying!

They are extremely convincing, and teachers, extended family, friends, etc. are all completely taken in. I understand about being scared to admit the truth, so I usually set out what will happen once we know the truth. Usually this does not work.

The most frustrating thing is that they lie in such a blatant way! I saw Sophie take Charley's bracelet. It was in her pocket, and yet she looked straight at me and swore blind she hadn't seen it. There was no need to lie about it. I took it out of her pocket and she said, 'Charley must have put it there to get me in trouble!'

The other day I came home and could smell that Charley had just made herself some toast. I don't mind her having a piece of toast but when I asked her about it she denied it completely even though it was still warm and in the bin! It's so frustrating. I mean what do they think I am going to do? I try to reassure them and spell out how I know, what the consequences are, etc., but they still completely deny everything in this really mad way!

Yesterday William told the teachers that he had no electricity in his room. I invited them round to check!

I think this is where it gets scary. I KNOW when the children are lying but other people don't. If they say I don't feed them, don't get them clothes, etc. some people *will* believe them. If ever they go to play with a friend, I catch the mums looking at me askance. I dread to think what they have been told.

I think it's the really pointless lies that I find the most tiring.

'No, I didn't have detention today.' They did.

'I found this £5 note in my bed.' It went missing from Rosie's purse.

'School is closed tomorrow.' I mean, really? Don't they think I will check?


## ☡ LIE OR DIE (Charley, 6 years; Sophie, 8 years; Katie, 10 years)

*I am a first-class liar and I tell lots of fibs.*
*I'm really quite different to most other kids.*
*I'm scared what will happen if I tell you the truth.*
*Will you beat me, reject me or just hit the roof?*

Sometimes I truly believe my own version,
And soon you'll agree without much coercion,
I'll make you doubt what you see with your eyes.
I'm a master deceiver with stories and lies.

I feel like I'm evil, wicked and bad.
I'm scared of the fallout and feel really sad.
I'm trying to protect me and keep myself safe,
And avoid that rejection I see in your face.

I feel so alone and I'm drowning in shame.
I quickly decide who else I can blame.
It's the only time I look into your eyes,
To make you believe there's truth in my lies.

You often demand that I have to be honest,
'But it just wasn't me,' I convincingly promise.
I've not nicked the money you've found in my pocket.
It fell out of the sky from an overhead rocket.

I say what I can to keep you on side.
I haven't got morals and what the hell's pride?
I just cannot link cause·and effect.
It's part of my brain that hasn't grown yet.

While you continue to stand and debate,
I've already decided what is my fate.
You're going to tell me to go pack my stuff.
I'm vile and disgusting and you've had enough.

Before you reject me and tell me to leave,
I've got another ACE up my sleeve.
Like a roaring lion that's escaped from its cage,
I go on the attack with uncontrolled rage.

*I'm so full of fear that you'll soon start to see*
*The hatred inside that I've got for me.*
*The look on your face just confirms what I know:*
*You really don't love me and now I must go.*

## ⬚ WILLIAM (9 years)

I can't help lying, I'm terrified of telling you the truth. What if you hurt me, reject me or see how disgusting I actually am? When I'm lying, my mouth is very dry and my lips stick together. Sometimes I lick them to make it easier for the words to come out. My tummy does somersaults all the while and I feel very, very hot.

There are times when I get confused about what the truth actually is and what happened where. Like the time I told the teachers that I didn't have electricity in my room. I'm sure this was true but Mummy said it's a lie. She was very upset and I couldn't really understand why.

## WHAT'S HAPPENING HERE?

Poor Sarah. She is struggling. She knows that this is probably a protective reflex, but even her best strategies seem to fail as her children persist in the lies that will keep them safe. It seems relentless, unnecessary and is so frustrating. If our children will not 'own up', how can they grasp cause and effect? How can we support and help them? Even the trivial things, such as lying about toast – what's that all about? It makes no sense, which is why we get so mad about it. Also, are we really so scary and horrid that we would refuse them the toast? What sort of person do they think we are? Do we look that stupid?

More worryingly though, what if these lies or half-truths lead to an allegation being made against us? This brings us to the other difficulty, which is usually described by parents as 'lack of respect'. The obvious, blatant nature of the lies makes us feel that we are being disrespected, and that seems to activate a really strong response. This is backed up by friends and family who helpfully tell us we cannot 'let them get away with it' or that we let our children 'walk all over us'. And part of us wonders if that might actually be true. The child, of course has a very different perspective.

Pervasive, toxic shame and fear are at the core of the child's behaviour.

The child has told a whopper, but the original behaviour is trauma-based (i.e. there has been food stolen, or a story made up to fit in, or an evasion) and this same traumatic root fuels the response – the absolute core knowledge, so clearly shown here and so heart-breaking, that this child is so convinced of their absolute worthlessness that they are sure that the slightest act will expose this true self to the world and that this will mean a further rejection, a further move, a further proof that they really are the bad child they already believe themselves to be.

So they lie to fit in, to avoid punishment (and who knows what punishment they may be expecting from their experiences). If they are confronted and pushed too far, the fear within them will escalate and produce a stress response, maybe resulting in a rage and violence out of all proportion to the offence.

Sometimes our children really struggle to distinguish the difference between lies, truth, what *happened* and what *is happening*.

## 🏆 REMEMBER...

- ✓ The child feels *pervasive, toxic shame*. I don't think it is easy for us to understand, but think of the experience of a toddler, just beginning to be told 'no'. It's the end of their world. They feel terrible shame. But, hopefully, they have the perceived rupture in the relationship repaired, they are given an explanation, and they are supported (see also Chapter 34, 'Shame').

✓ These three key tools help securely attached children separate their actions from themselves, so that they can see that the behaviour was wrong but they are still worthwhile and loved. Traumatised children may not have had this experience. They have not seen the wonder and love in a parent's eyes as they have developed. They have always been in the wrong. The shame of the experience is felt as part of their body – it relates to their feeling that they are so bad, and the shame is inescapable. This is pervasive shame.

## 🔖 TRY THIS…

✓ Avoid direct confrontation: Understand that this is so hard for the child.

✓ Empathise: Acknowledge the struggles that the child faces. Explain that you will help them get over the bumps and the bad times. You are not going anywhere. You understand it is scary because of their past.

✓ Nurture: Find ways to let them know you can 'see' their needs, and that you will help them.

✓ Repair ruptures: Let them know that doing something 'bad' does not mean they are bad. They have a good heart.

✓ Don't be afraid to make mistakes yourself, and to apologise if you get things wrong or make them fearful: This will model that everyone gets it wrong sometimes.

✓ Listen to them: Try to understand. Empathise with their perspective even if you don't agree and remember that hugs and nurture are unconditional. No buts.

✓ Reassure them: You are in this together. They are not moving on. You are family.

✓ Sometimes a 'lie' might come from the retrieval of a traumatic memory: The child has electricity in their room now, but maybe that was not always the case.

✓ Recognise the child's developmental age: Children with a developmental age of 3–6 years will tell incredible stories, and this is normal. Children who have trauma have different imaginings. Children with developmental trauma often have a lower developmental age than you would expect given their chronological age – for this reason, you may find children telling incredible and clearly untrue stories at a much later age. This disconnect between chronological age and developmental age is very difficult to manage, especially because our expectations of ability are closely linked to age and size.

## A FINAL INSIGHT

We have the privilege of letting the child speak for herself about how she experienced lying with the advantage of maturity and reflection.

## ⛉ WHAT YOU NEED TO DO (ROSIE)

> *My only hope is that that soon you will see*
> *It's all a result of what's happened to me.*
> *It isn't deliberate and it's not about you,*
> *It's a sad legacy from what I've been through.*
>
> *You need to just state that you know it's a lie,*
> *You know that I'm struggling and you'll figure out why.*

*Remind me you love me and I've got a good heart.*
*'Cos you're very aware of my difficult start.*

*Tell me I'm staying and I'm not moving on.*
*Though you're feeling quite sad with what I've done wrong,*
*Keep the consequence natural or as near as can be*
*Or maybe it's done more logically.*

*Whatever it is, be sure to see*
*It's bound up with nurture and real empathy,*
*As I need to build pathways deep in my brain*
*To link cause and effect without too much pain.*

*This all takes some time and is hard work for you,*
*But the more that you do it, the more you'll break through*
*To the small shattered heart that sits inside me*

*And the scared little child who needs a family.*
*Then my lies will reduce as I build up the trust*
*That it's not about me,*
*It's now about us.*

# 34

# **Shame**

Shame is a huge underlying factor for some of the most challenging behaviours we see in traumatised children. It is overwhelming for the child and we may see extreme reactions in order to avoid feeling shame.

Shame – or pervasive shame, which is inescapable – is affecting all the children, but in this chapter we see the impact on William.

## ✎ SARAH NAISH: Red ears

William is in trouble again at school. I've tried talking to him about it, but he just closes down. I know when he is feeling guilty because his ears go red. I'm not sure if that's shame, rage, embarrassment or anger. It's so hard to tell.

The school uses a reward chart system and I've tried explaining that this doesn't work for my children, but they just patronise me a bit more.

Sometimes when I have to confront William about something that has happened, it's so difficult. I try hard not to make him feel bad, but even if it's a really tiny thing he seems to be overwhelmed with this toxic shame.

We have had a serious issue with him running out of the class. I've tried to speak to him about it, but he just puts his head down and stares at the floor. The school is threatening to exclude him and have already put him in detention, but I just feel this is all WRONG!

I don't think he is trying to be bad. I think he is just reacting to whatever is in front of him. He seems to truly believe that he is a bad person and not worth anything. It doesn't matter what I say.

I do try to keep everything low key and give evidence to him about why he has a good heart. This works quite well although eye contact is non-existent. It's interesting how the children respond differently to shame: William closes down or runs away; Katie screams loudly; Charley and Rosie do loads of blaming, telling anyone who will listen how it's not their fault; and Sophie goes all blotchy and cries.

Last week I told him how clever he was for learning to tie his shoelaces, so he hasn't done it since! In fact, he pulled the laces right out of one of the shoes. It's almost like he is always trying to show me he is bad. It breaks my heart.

## ꧁ NOT A GOOD BOY (William, 10 years)

I can't seem to get things right. Some days I manage to remember how to do things and on other days I don't.

Last week I managed to tie my laces and Mummy was very proud of me. Now I can't do it but I don't want to ask her for help in case she is upset about it. Stupid, stupid laces!

It all got a bit tricky at school today. The teacher has a big picture of a rocket in the classroom. If we're good, we move the rocket up and get a prize on Friday. If we're bad, we move the rocket down. I don't know what happens on Friday if you're at the bottom. I'm doing my very best to stay at the top but I can't seem to concentrate on anything else except the rocket.

Connor fell over in the classroom and I laughed. I don't know why I laughed. I tried to hold it in but the laughter just came out anyway. Then I went all red and hot.

Miss James said I was unkind and should say sorry to Connor. I couldn't speak because my words had gone again, so Miss James sent me to Mrs Phillips. I felt a big feeling in my head and sick in my tummy. I don't want to be sick!

Mrs Phillips was very angry with me and I thought she might hurt me, so I ran out of the classroom and onto the field. I just ran and ran until I couldn't run anymore.

I wish I could just be a good boy and stop doing these silly things. I'm not good though. I'm not a good boy.

## WHAT'S HAPPENING HERE?

Shame is toxic. Shame is a horrible feeling that *you* are bad. It is not the same as guilt, which is easier to manage. Why is that? Well, shame is the name given to the awful gut-wrenching emotion we first experience as we learn to move around and start getting into trouble.

Our parents, who up until now have been delighted by our every move, gesture and attempt to engage them, suddenly get a horrid angry face and angry eyes and say 'NO!!' in a very loud voice. The child experiences an almost physical rupture and disintegrates into fearful tears. Their internal working model has suffered a disruption: maybe they are not wonderful anymore; their parents are unkind and scary; maybe they do not love them. Feelings of unbearable isolation flood their system. Then the parent reconnects with the child, co-regulates with them (cuddles and calms them down), assures them they are loved. They explain what has happened with a narrative: 'You really scared me. I thought you were going to fall down the stairs and get hurt!' From this, the child learns that they are still loved and important – it was the ACTION that was wrong.

Once this differentiation is assimilated, it becomes guilt – understanding that you were responsible for a wrong action. We call this task *'relationship repair'* and it is crucial for the development of resilience in relationships, as well as early moral concepts and understanding of rules when delivered consistently, predictably and reliably.

William suffered extreme abuse, including neglect, when his constant state of pain, fear, disconnect and experience of adults was terrifying; he had no experience of comfort, or the only time he was shown affection was when they allowed further abuse to happen, along with often a literal narrative of how bad he was through language and punishments.

This drives an internalisation of the fact that all the unbearable things that happen are because the child (William) is very bad. They may feel responsible for the adult's negative actions – it's their fault.

If a child like William who has had this experience is then disciplined, they will *know* that this is further proof of their bad nature, unless this is gently and patiently explained. They will be suffused with shame (turn red) and look at the floor to avoid angry eyes. They may laugh or smile – this is a common nervous tic and is perhaps a relic of a baby's attempts to appease and engage the adult. Other children respond differently – for example, Rosie's response is to blame others – or maybe there will be a crazy lie to act as protection.

## ☘ REMEMBER...

- ✓ Children who have toxic shame have missed out on vital developmental tools. They need to be supported with language and reassurance to make a different meaning.

Adults need to remember that the child who has not experienced empathy or relationship repair will not be able to express this towards others.

✓ Children who experience toxic shame have terror that relationships cannot be repaired as they have missed out on those vital relationship repair experiences.

✓ We need to avoid addressing shame-based behaviours with punitive consequences which will drive the child further into their condition, and instead gently help them to understand, and support them to show they are sorry or gain greater understanding. If we practise kindness and understanding, and model making mistakes and saying sorry, then the child will, in time, also develop these tools.

# 35

# **Violence**

In this section we look at the impact of aggression and child-to-parent violence. This is a much misunderstood, astonishingly common situation, which is subject to massive blame and condemnation by parents and children alike.

## ✎ SARAH NAISH: Aggression

The children aren't often violent – well, not *very* violent. I suppose there is a low-level constant aggression, with poking, pushing and blocking.

When Rosie was 8 years old, she was very aggressive. She thought nothing of pushing me and others aside, and would punch anyone who got in her way.

Sometimes I can just see that rage simmering. Everyone gives her a wide berth and tiptoes around her. I feel that it is almost bullying. I tend to confront it, but maybe that is not the right thing to do?

Rosie creates this brooding presence. The tension is so tight, you feel you could prick it like a balloon.

# ✎ SARAH NAISH: Violence

I know it's nowhere near as bad as for some other parents. I got this email today from my friend Emma. She adopted a child ten years ago and it puts my problems in perspective:

> *I am so scared. Where will it end? I have locked away the knives, taken down the pictures with glass in (after broken glass was used to self-harm). I have even moved the broom, the rolling pin and other easy weapons, but I cannot weapon-proof my house, and she always has her hands – my God, where does her strength come from? When I cry, it makes things worse. I have been strangled, kicked, punched and cut. How can I keep us both safe? Where is it going to end? What if she manages to kill me? No one is listening. My cuts and bruises are ignored, as are my black eyes. I feel like I am invisible. And if I restrain her, apparently I will be investigated for abuse. But I am the one being abused here.*

Today was about as bad as it gets for us. We had a full-blown attack on Katie. I have no idea where it came from. One minute we were sorting out the toy box, and the next minute Rosie had launched herself past me, pushing me out of the way (with a few choice expletives) to get at Katie.

Cue much hysterical screaming and shouting, with Rosie punching Katie in the head and chest as hard as she could. I managed to pull her off although I got punched too. I don't think she meant to. I don't think she knew what she was doing, to be honest.

Afterwards I tried to get to the bottom of it, and apparently Katie had 'said something nasty' which Rosie could not even remember!

I tried unpicking it and talking about taking a deep breath to help her calm down, etc., but Rosie just gave me one of her scathing 'you are an imbecile' looks.

I am not scared of Rosie but I can see a lot of people are. When she sticks her chin out, with that determined look on her face, she looks very powerful. I don't know how we will manage as she gets bigger and stronger. I have not been taught the strategies to put in place to keep everyone safe. My biggest fear is that I will accidentally hurt someone as I try and break up a fight. Last week a social worker told me not to touch them if they were having a fight. I don't think I have ever actually heard anything so stupid. I did explain that one of them had taken the dog lead and was trying to strangle the other, but she just looked at me like I was exaggerating. I wasn't.

I am damned if I intervene and damned if I don't.

## I'LL GET HER! (Rosie, 13 years)

Why does she always say 'no'. I'm fed up with it. Katie always gets her own way. Stupid idiot!

I will get my own back – I'll make sure of it. I told Mummy to get out of my way and called her a big fat cow. Katie poked her nose in, so I punched her. I punched her over and over again until Mummy pulled me off her. I think Mummy got a few punches as well. I can't quite remember, but it serves her right if she did. It's all a bit of a blur really. Strange how I often forget what actually happened when I'm that angry. All I know is: it wasn't my fault. I often feel angry, I'm not really sure why, but the anger gets so big that I can't control it. It's like riding my bike down a hill without any brakes!

One minute I feel mostly OK, and the next I feel like killing someone. I'm not going to kill anyone though. I certainly hope

I don't. That would be really bad. Am I really bad? I must be to think that.

I think I'm actually a bit scared but I'm not going to tell anyone that as they'll think I'm a pushover.

I'm not a pushover, I'm strong. I have to be strong. I have to protect myself. I don't trust anyone else to protect me. Why would they? There are times when I've hit someone and I didn't even mean to. There's a big whooshy feeling in my arms and feet, and before I know it I've bashed someone. I do feel that horrible hot feeling afterwards but it does get a bit better once I've been shouted at. I wonder why I like being shouted at sometimes. Perhaps I deserve it.

I do so wish I could stop and think before I hit people, throw stuff or break things. But I just can't. Even if I think it, my arms do it anyway.

I am so tired. Katie looks scared. I think she has been crying. I can't remember what happened. I know I was stressed and angry. I'm not angry now but I really need a sleep. I can never remember what has happened when I am angry but I know it is bad. I think I am a really terrible person. That makes me so stressed and angry all over again. I can see that Katie has bruises. Did I do that? I don't want to hurt anyone. Why does it keep happening? I know Sarah hates me now. She is going to get rid of me soon, I know it. No one loves me. They all hate me really. I can't cope, I am so stressed. I want to go and die in a hole.

## WHAT'S HAPPENING HERE?

In these two stories, we have two different levels of violence. The underlying cause is the same, but the degree of stress is different. The behaviour stems from the fight/flight response, where in the face of a threat to survival you fight, run for your life or freeze into immobility to avoid being noticed. The response will be determined by your earliest experiences and what worked for you then.

## Stress hormones

The difference between the levels of violence here results from the level of stress hormones (cortisol and adrenaline) in the system. The abnormally high levels of stress trigger additional release of adrenaline which is specifically released as part of the fight/flight response (cortisol is produced as a result of chronic ongoing stress, affecting changes in blood glucose levels, whereas adrenaline is a direct response to sudden acute stress and danger). Very often, traumatised children have high levels of cortisol in their system, even when their system is at rest. Often this is triggered by a pre-birth experience, such as high levels of cortisol in the mother's bloodstream due to domestic violence, extreme poverty or a hidden pregnancy. The overall effect is that it takes very small additional amounts of stress to trigger a disproportionate response, which seems to come from nowhere. To check if your child has high levels of circulating cortisol, just look at their eyes. When circulating cortisol is high, the pupils dilate.

## Aggression

The abnormally high levels of cortisol create a situation when the child is quickly roused to angry reactions. Small triggers activate the amygdala, sending danger signals to the central nervous system. The capability of the prefrontal cortex to integrate and respond appropriately is compromised because in the child's experience small issues such as hunger or lack of parental attention are indicators of an imminent threat which needs to be dealt with immediately.

## Violence

Unbridled and terrifying attacks with or without a weapon occur when the child has reached a point of overwhelm where there is no longer any thought process involved. In this case the amygdala has been triggered to an extent which disrupts the ability of the cortex to rationalise or to control impulse; or it may be that a small incident has triggered a massive survival response because the amygdala has been firing all day over smaller stressors, and the cortex cannot maintain functionality. Either way, at this point the cortex is disengaged in order to allow the child to fully utilise the fight/flight system to save themselves. Taking time to think and process costs precious moments that can make the difference between life or death. In this state it is perfectly possible for violence to occur and for the child to have no recollection, or to recall in the form of flashbacks (a symptom of post-traumatic stress disorder (PTSD)).

## 🏆 REMEMBER...

- ✓ Our traumatised children have massive stress. They have a negative perspective of themselves and the world. They fight to survive. The stress response is always near the surface.

- ✓ For a child whose earliest needs were not met, hunger, pain cold or lack of attention are truly a threat to survival. It will take years and patience to create new understanding and 'rewire' the brain (i.e. create new neurological pathways in the cortex).

## 🪶 TRY THIS...

- ✓ Remember it is not the child but the *experiences* the child has had that drive the behaviour.

- ✓ Look for early warning signals and be prepared to de-escalate early on.

- ✓ There are very few courses available to manage violent behaviour in traumatised children that teach de-escalation and safe physical intervention which maintains the relationship. However, 'Managing Violent Behaviour' is a two-part, face-to-face course based on therapeutic parenting principles, but also has part one available online. For details, please visit the Inspire Training Group website at www.inspiretraininggroup.com.

# 36

# School

Very often, school feels overwhelmingly difficult for children who have experienced trauma. The parent's experience is often extremely difficult too. School seems to be fraught with problems for all the children. This isn't easy for anyone, least of all Sarah, who is trying to tread a fine line.

✎ SARAH NAISH: School fail!

There is no doubt about it: school has been a complete nightmare from start to finish.

At infant and junior school the Local Authority thought it would be helpful if the children all went to different schools! Oh yes, because that would be really great for drop-off and pick-up times!

Then we had all the issues about school trips and reward charts. I made sure the school knew about William's traumatic background, but they still insisted it would be fine to take him on a school visit to some dark caves with scary wax figures. I did try to tell them what would happen (the teacher looked quite pale when they returned).

Every school has been fixated on reward charts and detentions. Detentions are complete rubbish. Often the school forgets that they have set them. Rosie did actually manage to get to one last week, only to find that there was no one there!

I've had letters about packed lunches, telling me what I should and should not put in them. They did not believe me when I said that often the children eat their lunches on the way to school if they are not closely supervised.

We did have an absolutely brilliant teacher once. I know William felt safe with her. I felt he could finally relax and start to learn. There was minimum disruption and the teacher kept everything consistent and predictable. I wish every school was like that.

The move to secondary school has been a big fail for each child so far. None of them could cope with the classroom changes. They would 'get lost' or simply leave the building!

Even though I worked hard to get education 'statements' for all the children, setting out their individual needs, these were largely ignored. On one occasion, Rosie had a meltdown in art and pushed her teacher into a cupboard! Although, of course, that was absolutely not OK, the school set her up to fail. She was supposed to have proper warning and preparation if a new teacher was coming in, but they sent in a supply teacher with no warning at all, then wondered why she went off on one! I swear they just *want* to exclude my children!

As for homework... Well, I just stopped any pretence at trying to do that about two years in. It was a constant battle and I didn't feel it was helping the children, or me, in any way. I suppose that makes me a bad parent too. Oh well – sorry... not sorry. Oh dear, I am beginning to sound like the children.

## TRAUMA BURPS (William, 10 years)

*I've got a tricky problem,*
*I call it 'trauma burps'.*

*They come up from my tummy*
*and say some nasty words.*

*They burped out to my teacher*
*'Cos she was in my way.*
*Now I've got detention*
*But I feel too scared to stay.*

*The Head asked why I do it, and I said,*
*'I DON'T KNOW WHY.'*
*She said I need to STOP IT,*
*And now I want to cry.*

*I don't dislike my teacher,*
*but her glasses make me wobble.*
*That's why I called her ugly*
*And it's gotten me in trouble.*

*Trauma burps are awful,*
*You don't know when they'll happen.*
*The adults say I'm 'naughty',*
*And that makes me want to slap 'em.*

*Maybe I have got them*
*'Cos I'm a rotten kid.*
*I didn't mean to say it,*
*But the teacher said I did.*

*Deep down in my tummy*
*I feel those dreaded burps,*
*So Mum said she would help*
*As they may be from past hurts.*

*She gave me a big cuddle*
*And I felt the burpies pop.*
*Perhaps I might believe*
*She can help to make them stop.*

*She thinks I got the trauma burps*
*When I was very small,*
*And they bounce round in my tummy*
*Especially at school.*

*She's going to tell the teacher*
*I'm not a 'naughty lad',*
*I didn't mean to say it*
*And burps are when I'm sad.*

I'm always getting into trouble at school. I do try to be good but most of the time I'm just trying to get through the day. There are lots of different teachers and I feel scared. I don't tell them that, though; I just pretend I don't care. I just don't trust adults one little bit and there are so many of them at school. Sometimes they have supply teachers and they're even more scary as I don't know them and I'm not sure what they might do. I miss my mummy when I'm at school. I wonder if she ever thinks about me when I'm there? Will she remember to pick me up? What if she doesn't come back at the end of the day?

The school day is very long and I don't like moving from one class to another – I much prefer it when we stay in the same classroom. Mr Johnson's classroom has a big light in the ceiling and it flickers all the time. It makes my head feel fizzy. He also has a big shouty voice and he makes me jump. I hope he doesn't hurt me. When teachers shout, I get really scared as it reminds me of adults shouting when I was little. I wonder if I'm going to get hit, so I often hit them first.

When we go to the dinner hall, the other children push and shove me in the corridor, and sometimes I punch them or run away and hide somewhere. Will I be able to get seconds of dinner? I might just say that Mummy doesn't feed me. When I said this last week, Mrs Taylor gave me extra chips.

I don't like playtime either. I don't really know how to play the games the other kids are playing. If I try to join in, they say I'm ruining their game. I usually play on my own or just walk around the playground making those noises that usually get me into trouble.

The teachers try to set me up by putting my name on the good side of the board now and again. They know I'm not good, so why try to pretend I am? It just doesn't sit right with me. I soon make sure I'm back where I belong – either on the sad side or sat outside the Headteacher's office. I quite like it there though, as it's far less noisy and she keeps an eye on me.

Kevin can't get me if the Head is watching me.

## I'M NOT DOING HOMEWORK (William, 11 years)

*Why do I have to do stupid homework?*
*I've done enough work at school,*
*Keeping myself really quiet*
*Or breaking every rule.*

*Either way you look at it,*
*It's not been that much fun.*
*I can't cope with you being my teacher*
*As well as being my mum.*

*My relationships are far more important*
*Than ridiculous, pointless SATS*
*Or tests that I'll fail anyway,*
*And so what if I'm crap at Maths?*

*If I don't rewire my brain,*
*Which only YOU can help me do,*
*I'll remain in survival mode*
*And continue to feel like poo.*

*School is such a scary place,*
*So noisy and so busy,*
*I honestly cannot concentrate*
*'Cos my head feels really fizzy.*

*When I come home I want to leave*
*School outside the door.*
*I know I'm 11 in real life*
*But actually I'm 4!*

## WHAT'S GOING ON HERE?

School presents many problems for William (or any other child who has suffered trauma). The good bits (structure, routine and predictability) are massively outweighed by the social, emotional and cognitive demands placed on William.

Many of the children we see who have experienced trauma have not developed the neurological patterns to enable them to cope emotionally and socially, even if they are cognitively very able. In addition, many children have suffered physical damage to their developing brain structure as a result of (for example) alcohol or drug misuse, or they may have suffered brain damage due to physical abuse or a difficult birth experience. As a result, they may have learning difficulties which can be lifelong and hidden, so school does not see them properly.

High cortisol levels keep our children on high alert. This literally impedes their ability to hear, never mind process or link ideas constructively. Children report experiencing buzzing noises in their ears that stop them hearing. The loud, chaotic busy school environment and difficulties in managing social and other interactions increases cortisol production due to stress, making the situation even harder to manage (see also Chapter 21, 'Hypervigilance').

In order to learn, the child needs first to be absolutely aware that their physiological needs are met, so that they do not even have to think about these. They have to feel safe so that they can focus on something other than their environment and the movements and actions of the pupils and teachers (especially teachers due to a complete mistrust of adults). They also have to feel like they belong. Only then are they able to engage in exploration and therefore learning. The harsh reality for our children is that often they are unable to disengage from their fears and their past experiences, which means they are often delayed in social and emotional areas. Executive function (see Chapter 31, 'Memory') has not developed, so there is reduced or absent ability to process and follow instructions, self-regulate or have any impulse control. Enhanced activation of the survival areas of the brain, triggered by multiple stressors throughout the day, leads to overwhelm and stressed impulsive reactions as described above. Punitive methods of discipline induce shame, fear and escalation. This leads to further adverse labelling of the child.

## Homework

The problem with homework is that it is often a step too far for the children. Here is why.

Firstly, they have been struggling with the immense demands of school all day and they need time to process and to rest. Sometimes the child's level of stress when first getting home requires the parent to spend time reconnecting with and regulating them, using reassurance and exercise or other strategies. To then ask them to sit and do homework reignites their stress, with the result that more disruptive incidents occur.

Secondly, these children are performing early developmental tasks around social and emotional development, mediated by their family. They are learning about relationships and trust, and trying to manage the huge leap into vulnerability that will enable them to adjust their negative internal working model. This is a big job and is necessary for lifelong relationships to be possible. It is the ongoing work of the parents and child together. This is their 'home' work.

Thirdly, very often our children cannot manage to do tasks that belong to school at home, due to rigid or black-and-white thinking (which is typical of much younger children). To try to force this issue causes massive arguments and distress, which interrupt the vital work the parents are doing in other areas.

Finally, there are examples of research both for and against the homework debate. In the case of children from trauma, except in some rare cases, homework is non-productive and creates huge conflict at home which is clearly of no benefit to parents or child. Taking a child-centred approach to this will enable each child to work within their capability.

## ♀ REMEMBER...

- ✓ A child who has suffered trauma will take time to heal – sometimes years.

## ♣ TRY THIS...

- ✓ A quiet, calm environment helps reduce anxiety.

- ✓ Change the environment to support the child – make the classroom less busy and seat the child to support their needs.

- ✓ Seek professional training to help understand developmental trauma and develop strategies (see http://inspire traininggroup.com).

- ✓ Keep in mind that, as the parent, you are the most valuable source of information about your child.

# 37

# Isolation

Many parents of traumatised children or children with additional needs tell us that they have never felt more lonely and disconnected from friends and family than when they are coping with extreme behaviours at home. It is a common experience as Sarah is discovering here.

## ✎ SARAH NAISH: Lonely

I am sitting here looking out of the window at the trees. I don't think I've ever felt more alone in my whole life.

The children's behaviours mean that friends and family don't want to visit us and definitely don't want us to visit them! It makes it worse when they try to give me parenting tips, because they really don't understand that my children need a different type of parenting.

When I try to explain this, they just patronise me and give me examples of their own parenting and how great they are. I sit there in my little bubble, alone, frustrated and feeling like everyone around me is speaking a different language.

I remember back to when I was being assessed to adopt the children and recall with some hilarity the eco-map that we did. What a joke that was! Everyone who was on it is either no longer there, or they think we are a family who needs 'intervention'.

Some of them are people whom I smile at hopefully, thinking maybe they will give me a break. They don't give me a break, because they just think my children are badly behaved and they don't know what to do.

They remember things like William coming out of school day after day with wet trousers. I remember the tips they tried to give me on potty training. He was 9 years old.

They remember the time when Rosie was invited for a play date but literally ate all the pies. I did tell them not to do a 'help-yourself tea'. They didn't listen. They said I was too strict. So now they just don't invite us, so they can be right and ignore the mistake they made.

My friend Lucy remembers the time when Katie went for the day and would not leave her baby alone. Literally, she could not step away. Katie's experience is that babies get hurt, babies might die. She was protecting the baby. My friend felt threatened. She hasn't offered to help again and always visits without her children now. She looks at my children warily and asks questions about 'therapy'.

So, the children are badly behaved, they have 'special needs' and I'm a bad parent.

We are the family to avoid.


## ⭒ AUNTY DRAGON (Rosie, 14 years)

Mummy took us to visit our uncle, aunt and cousin today. I hate visiting new people. Charley didn't stop talking the whole time we were in the car and Mummy couldn't hear the radio.

William had wet himself by the time we arrived. Everyone was causing arguments except me.

Uncle Jim asked if we had enjoyed the countryside on our way here. What countryside?

I said I wanted a biscuit. Aunty Jenny put five on a plate. I ate them all. Mummy was busy sorting out William and Charley. Sophie was very quiet and Katie was pretending to be nice. She was a bit upset when she realised I'd eaten all of the biscuits though.

The cousin kept trying to speak to me but I told her to go away. She started to cry. I think she's spoilt anyway. Her parents obviously love her more than mine ever loved me. She has everything!

Uncle Jim looks a bit angry and Aunty Jenny is breathing loudly through her nose. I think she looks like a dragon. I don't like dragons.

I think I need more biscuits. I ask Aunty Jenny if I can have some more. Strangely enough, her dragon breathing gets louder and she doesn't answer me. I really don't like visiting new people.

## WHAT'S HAPPENING HERE?

This chapter is very much about the consequences for the parent from the behaviour of their children. Everyone has an opinion! Parents report trying and trying to help friends and family understand, only to face greater disconnect than ever. In the end, they give up, retreating with their families into a smaller and smaller social space.

The children in the example above are only behaving as they are hardwired to do as a result of their experiences. Unfortunately, many extended family members and friends seem to think that as soon as the child is with the 'safer' parents, or that a trauma has passed, it is like the parent has a magic wand to make it better.

# ℞ TRY THIS...

- ✓ See if your family and friends will accept information and education about this.

- ✓ Try to help them to understand – the earlier the better.

- ✓ Let them know how they can support you, and how valuable this is.

- ✓ The National Association of Therapeutic Parents has fact sheets you can print out to give to family and friends who struggle to understand (www.naotp.com).

## A message to friends and family

Never tell the parent of a traumatised child that it happened when they were so young and they won't remember. Children may not have a narrative memory, but their body remembers and their brains respond in ways that are adapted to past experiences. That's how brains work. Children need multiple positive experiences to rewire their brains and create new ideas and a new understanding. It's hard, it takes a long time.

It's hard to stay out of blame and judgement. It is easy to be scared for your friend, your sibling, child, niece or nephew. Take the time to learn – there are lots of resources and places to look. You can dismiss your friend/relative and decide that their parenting is at fault, the child is at fault, or it's all someone else's fault. The parents are already struggling and you will become just one more person who blames them. They will probably withdraw.

Your unconditional support and love is gold to parents and children alike. The few people who stay with therapeutic parents on the journey are their anchors.

# 38

# **Guilt**

Sometimes the person who has the highest expectation of ourselves is us! And when we fail to live up to our own unrealistic expectations, we feel awful. This is how Sarah is feeling here, but her child seems unaware!

## ✎ SARAH NAISH: Failed

I've blown it again!

I can't believe that she is so able to make me lose my temper. I know it's not her fault and I should not blame her.

I am the one at fault here. I am the adult and I am the one who is supposed to be the 'unassailable safe base'. It's so hard being on my own though with no break!

Well I was NOT very unassailable today. In fact, the children were all over me like ants! I just feel like I can't do it sometimes. Everything is going so well and then there is one comment or expression, one more bit of ungratefulness and I just snap!

I said things I don't mean. What if she always remembers that? I told her to get out. She didn't seem to care but I REJECTED HER!

I sometimes feel I am not fit to be any parent, let alone a therapeutic parent.

I have come to bed now, feeling miserable and hollow inside. I don't know how to put this right; and the hardest thing is knowing that whatever I do will probably make it worse. What if I am actually damaging my children? What if I can't do it after all?

Feeling hopeless and like a failure.

## WHAT'S WRONG? (Rosie, 14 years)

I don't know what's wrong with Mummy today. She's been acting a bit weird.

We all had a big fight this morning, which I got blamed for (as usual). Mummy got a bit shouty. I can't even remember what she was shouting about or even what she said.

Everybody was being very loud and arguing about what to watch on the telly. Charley was making stupid noises and someone punched her. It was not me!

Sophie told William that we wouldn't be getting any sweets and he started to cry. Katie was eating the biscuits she'd hidden up her jumper. I was trying to sort everything out.

Mummy told me to leave, so I walked to the end of the road and spoke to my friends on the corner. We all shared a big bag of crisps one of them had bought from the corner shop.

It all seemed pretty normal to me, but Mummy said it's been an awful day. I have no idea what she's talking about. We still had dinner and we even got the sweets. For some unknown reason, we actually got extra sweets!

Mummy said she was very sorry for being so nasty and telling me to leave. How weird is that?! Adults are strange. Doesn't she realise that the worst day with her is like heaven compared to living with Jackie and Kevin!

## WHAT'S HAPPENING HERE?

Poor Sarah – she has fallen into the parent trap. The relentless nature of therapeutic parenting (especially with a group of siblings with individual needs, issues and responses to trauma) has induced a disproportionate reaction to her very understandable inability to attain perfection.

When we enter into the world of therapeutic parenting, we make a pledge to ourselves that we will be the ones that will make the difference to our new family. We attend all the training, we fill in our form F, we lay bare the deepest reaches of our soul, and we prove that we will be a perfect parent, no matter what challenges face us. For foster parents there is a very similar process, and the same commitment. However, nothing prepares us for the 24/7 reality of managing to parent a deeply traumatised child or children. When we are pushed to our very limits and respond 'untherapeutically', the guilt we feel is immense – we feel that we have failed, that we are not good enough, and worst of all we fear that we are replicating the original trauma.

It is very interesting to read the child's perspective – that it's all over and done with, and anyway that was normal, wasn't it? In fact, it was way better than 'normal' used to be!

## ♟ REMEMBER...

- ✓ Here's the thing: Thinking about what is 'normal' is a very subjective thing to do. In fact, our children unconsciously replicate scripts that lead to parental explosions – that level of chaos feels 'normal' to them.

- ✓ As the Introduction to this book, which describes the metaphor of Rooms 1 and 2, makes clear, the child's un-processed memories and feelings around their previous experience (Room 1) can hijack them at any time. Finding the way through this maze requires knowledge of their history, therapeutic parenting, unbelievable amounts of patience and the ability to forgive yourself. That's a big ask.

## The good news...

The good news is that relationships repair. Throughout childhood, we need to separate behaviour from self – i.e. tricky behaviour does not mean you are bad. It means you made a mistake or a poor choice.

The other lesson children take from these numerous ruptures in their connection with their parents is that love survives arguments – it is resilient. Adults can get angry for a variety of reasons – for example, fear (the children were about to run in the road or play with the fire), stress (the parent is too busy to deal with something else right now), etc. – but they can make amends and say, 'Sorry I shouted.'

Make amends with your child with a small gesture of kindness. Parents model this so that the children can learn. Thus, the good news is, your occasional loss of temper is not the end of the world. It is an opportunity to say sorry, to teach and to become stronger as a result.

# 39

# Therapy

Many families pin all their hopes on getting the 'right therapy' for their child. Sadly these hopes often come crashing down around their ears. There is no magic wand which 'fixes' traumatised children.

The family's experience of therapy is varied. It feels like Sarah was hoping this would be a magic solution to some of Katie's difficulties. Is it though?

## ✎ SARAH NAISH: Mental health professionals

Over the years we have been to Child and Adolescent Mental Health Services (CAMHS) a number of times. This has been occasionally helpful and usually not. Family therapy was the funniest. The psychiatrist kept talking about milk bottles being full and spilling out with anger. This worked the first time but by the seventh it got a bit repetitive! The only positive was that Rosie and I always exchanged amused glances, trying not to laugh!

Then there was the child psychiatrist who suggested Katie just needed to go horse riding and all her issues would be resolved.

We had one brilliant mental health nurse though, who came to meetings at the school and actually understood child trauma. That was such a relief!

Now it's been decided that Katie is going to see a psychologist on her own. Not sure how this will go!

## Before the appointment

Finally, the appointment has come through. They are going to start off with Katie, but I am bit worried as they insist on seeing her on her own. I know she gets mixed up with what has happened and what nearly happened. Hopefully, the therapist is very skilled. I have written and said I think I need to come in at least for part of the appointment.

Katie is cross now about having to go. She thought she was going to be able to miss school and it turns out the appointment is at 4 pm, so now she doesn't want to go. Rosie is very cross that she is not going first, and her behaviour has deteriorated. We definitely have Rosie Rudey in the house!

## After the appointment

Well that was fun (not)!

Juggling the childcare so I could attend the appointment was a challenge. They seemed to think it would be OK for me and the other four children to all sit outside the room and amuse ourselves.

I know I was hoping for a magic fix but I can see that was another futile dream.

When Katie came out, it was very clear she had played the therapist. She had managed to extract some sweets and had told a story about our dog dying, which was not true.

I cannot see how this can work if I am not there to help ground her, but apparently I am a nobody. I know nothing and I have to allow Katie to confuse fantasy and reality.

Surely this cannot help any of us?

## ⊰ GET OUT OF MY HEAD! (Katie, 12 years)

### Before the appointment

I have to go to therapy. Does this mean I'm crazy? None of my friends have to go to see a therapist. It's really scary being in a room all by myself with a strange adult. She looks OK but she's a bit too nice. It makes me feel unsafe. I don't know her yet but she's being so friendly. What does she want?

Is she going to make me talk about stuff I don't want to think about? I need to make her like me. I need to keep myself safe. I'll tell her that Mummy doesn't feed me. Maybe she'll give me food. If she feels sorry for me, she won't hurt me.

### At the appointment

The therapist talks to me like I'm a good person. I'm not a good person – can't she see that? I'm a bad kid. If I wasn't bad, I wouldn't need therapy!

I wish my mummy was in the room with me. She said she'd keep me safe. She's outside in the waiting room and I don't feel bloody safe. I think my mummy has lied to me.

My legs feel all wobbly and I need the loo. I cross my legs and try to hold it in.

I can feel a smile forming at the edges of my mouth. I'm not happy, so I know it's not a real smile. I'm not sure what a real smile is, but this one isn't even a fake one!

Lots of questions about what I like to do, how I feel, how things are going at school. I haven't got a clue. I just want to go home.

I give her the answers I think she wants to hear so I can get out of here. We do some drawing and make a dog out of play-doh. I told her I like dogs – that was a bit true – but seriously, how old does she think I am? Play-doh?!

I know she's trying to get into my head. I don't let anyone into my head. Not even my mummy.

Why does she think I'll let her in?

## WHAT'S HAPPENING HERE?

Getting an appointment with CAMHS is usually hard. Parents may have high hopes or, as here, the parent has some trepidation.

Katie is clearly not in the same place though! Unfortunately, sometimes the child is seen alone. Although rarely and exceptionally this may be appropriate, as a rule this is where the problems start. Traumatised children do not have a good understanding of what has happened to them; often they just have very confused feelings. However, they do know they need to appease the adult (whom they do not trust) as much as possible. They mask their fear, plastering a smile on their face, nodding their agreement – yes, they know why they are there; yes, it's fine to ask questions – but inside they are deeply mistrustful of all adults, including the one in front of them right now. Adults do not care. There must be a bad reason for all this niceness. Better keep on the right side of them.

The children have survived, and they keep using the same techniques that have allowed them to stay alive. The fear and stress emerges once they get home, which sometimes reinforces the view that clearly the parents need some help with how to use good parenting strategies.

Asking for information from the children is deeply triggering for them. It puts them back into their fear (Room 1). What might happen if they tell? Or they may become confused: which mummy are we talking about?

The other question is one of relationships. The children are barely able to manage to accommodate *our* attempts to connect. Asking them to embark on a new trusting relationship – one which will inevitably end – puts a massive strain on them and on us. It is detrimental to the development of the child to ask them to manage this new dependency.

They will not know how to manage, and they will project their own feelings and fears onto their parents: 'I don't think she cares about me' and 'Mummy shouts a lot and I get scared'. There may be further damage to the home relationship: 'At least my therapist cares about me. You don't!'

There are models of therapeutic intervention such as Dyadic Developmental Psychotherapy (DDP)[1] and Theraplay®[2] which work through the child–parent relationship, and these have proven to be extremely effective when working with traumatised children.

## 🏆 REMEMBER...

- ✓ Our children need to establish a secure relationship with the safe parent *before* they are asked to embark on a secondary one.

- ✓ As a therapeutic parent, you must be present during sessions to offer support, empathy and comfort. This reinforces your position as a safe base for the child.

- ✓ You should have access to the therapist before the sessions (to give a background), during (to clear up any mis-interpretation), and after (to reflect and discuss ways forward).

---

1   DDP was developed in 2000 by Dan Hughes and associates and is a child and relationship based approach. It recognises that the extremely challenging behaviours displayed by some children are the only way they can express the anxiety that emerges when they are parented, and even more so with a standard parenting approach. The technique uses PACE (an attitude of Playfulness, Acceptance, Curiosity and Empathy) as the cornerstone of the approach.
2   Theraplay is defined by the Theraplay Institute as 'a child and family therapy for enhancing attachment, self-esteem, trust in others and joyful engagement'. Theraplay sessions guide families to provide opportunities for connection, regulation and trust using a variety of activities.

✓ Traumatised children need to keep adults under their control. They misinform – not always deliberately, but they may nonetheless give false information because they will talk about their fears and not reality (e.g. 'My mum really had a go at me about...') and this will lead to 'splitting'[3] and a distraction of the therapy away from its true purpose. Remember that fact and fiction, past and present, are very confused for the child with developmental trauma.

✓ Finally, remember that you are the expert on your child. You need to be part of the process, especially since you, as a therapeutic parent, are the regulatory presence for your traumatised child. Therapy is good, but it must be the RIGHT therapy and the safe parent MUST be informed and involved.

---

3    'Splitting' or triangulation occurs when there are several agencies working with the same child and the child controls the information flow by insisting (for example) that parents do not go into therapy sessions. This enables the child to control the whole situation and can provoke 'splitting' of the professionals, teachers and parents preventing coherent teamwork.

# 40

# **Always on the Move**

Children who have suffered developmental trauma often have very high circulating cortisol. This is like their body being on full alert all the time with a pounding heart and feelings of being agitated and not being able to keep still.

If the child is feeling extra anxious, this triggers further cortisol production and makes matters worse. Because the central nervous system interprets a threat, the body is taking over from the brain, making sure that the body is ready to manage the challenge and run or fight, keeping the child wakeful and alert with eyes and ears wide open for signs of danger.

Sarah's family is starting to struggle with the high cortisol levels everywhere. This makes for a busy and stressful environment.

✎ SARAH NAISH: Annoying

The constant movement, talking and tapping drives me mad sometimes!

If we are all sitting on the sofa together, they can't just sit quietly and watch television, even if I'm sitting in the room. Their feet will be tapping on the floor, and their hands will be picking holes in the sofa, their clothes, or just poking each other. I think the inability to relax and sit still also contributes to all the damage that happens, especially with clothing, bedding, etc.

There is a constant background noise of tapping, scraping, screeching or silly noises and other annoying sounds.

William can't just have a shower. He has a shower while making weird noises. The banging and breaking noises which come out of the shower room are quite worrying at times! He needs to open and close the shower door while he is *in* the shower, because just being in the shower does not seem to be 'busy enough'!

Car journeys are the worst. I have to be very creative to keep the children occupied and busy, almost like you would with a toddler. I've actually come to the conclusion that they can't sit still. It is a physical impossibility.

My friends say they think they have ADHD, but I don't believe this. I think there is something much deeper going on. How come I can manage it at home with structure and routines, but everyone else seems to struggle?

I've noticed as well, what goes along with this is their inability to concentrate. This is really tiring because it means that they can't relax and read a book; and even when they are watching a film, there will be the need to disrupt that or to fidget, get up and down several times, or just ask questions all the way through it.

The words 'chillout' and 'relax' don't seem to exist anymore in our house. The trampoline comes in useful. That uses up a lot of their energy and they like bouncing on it (constantly), but I wonder if there will ever be a day when we all sit in the same room and just relax together. That feels like a distant dream.

## I CAN'T SIT STILL (William, 11 years)

I can't sit still. I feel very wobbly and the only way I can feel a bit less wobbly is to keep moving. I don't even realise I'm doing it until an adult points it out – usually by telling me to stop fidgeting, sit still, listen and concentrate. I can't, I just can't. Charley can't stop talking and I can't sit still. Sometimes, I feel like I've got a rushing feeling in my head and it makes me all hot and sticky. I need to get it out.

Mummy likes us to have 'quiet time' together – reading or quiet play. I can't stand the quiet. I feel very scared, like something really bad is going to happen. I need the noise to feel better.

I get very wobbly in the shower. What if they forget about me when I'm up there, or even leave me? I make lots of noise to remind them that I'm there. I also need to remind myself.

I can easily forget what I'm doing or where I am, so I open and shut the shower door. It reminds me that I'm in the shower. I often wonder what's going on downstairs and if I make lots of noise, Mummy comes to check on me and I feel a little bit better. I'm worried I'll become invisible if I stop making a noise.

Car journeys are worse though. I feel really worried about where we are going. Am I going back to the people who hurt me? Am I being taken to live somewhere else? Also, Mummy has her eyes on the road and I'm worried she's forgotten me. I have a little sweet to suck as Mummy thinks it might help. I can't keep it in my mouth though. I usually roll it around the seat. It makes lovely sticky patterns. If I haven't got a sweet, I usually chew my jumper. I like chewing stuff. I like having something in my mouth. It really does make the wobblies less wobbly.

## WHAT'S GOING ON HERE?

The children are suffering from the neurological, emotional, physiological and physical effects of developmental trauma. The trauma occurs as a result of not having had an attuned relationship with an adult from birth. This may of course be to a greater or lesser extent, but in children who have suffered severe abuse and neglect it is extreme. The effect of this is that their experiences have activated 'wiring' in their brain (neurological connections and pathways in their cortex), leading them towards fear and survival instead of trust and exploration. There was no rhyme nor reason to their experiences, so their thinking may be chaotic. They trust things instead of adults to help them.

These children have extremely high circulating cortisol because of the stress that they have endured. Their stress from life is extremely high – their expectation is that at any moment they may be in danger, because this has been their experience. Their systems are on high alert, and they have physiological symptoms, often described as wobbly feelings, or a whooshy feeling in their tummy, or a buzzing in their ears.

As their body responds to their fears and triggers which are unknown to us, they are flooded with adrenaline, which increases blood supply to their heart, lungs and muscles, getting them ready to run or fight. Their feet get tippy tappy, they feel agitated, they pick or chew at clothing. This is a physical response.

Their emotional state is perpetually fearful, and as stress levels rise, so does their fear – of being alone, invisible, ignored – these were survival issues for them. So they chatter, bang and crash to give themselves a sensation of not being alone and to bring their parent's attention to them. In addition, children who have not had sensory stimulation are sensory-seeking. They need to fill the development gap. So they jump, bang, push or chew.

It is impossible for these children to relax, to concentrate, to focus. They *are* concentrating and focusing – on surviving. That is far more pressing a need than enjoying a film, listening to instructions or processing a lesson.

# ♟ REMEMBER...

- ✓ We need to help our children fill their developmental gaps. We can reframe these behaviours and remember they are attention needing, not attention seeking. We can help them to manage their feelings by noticing their states and by using therapeutic parenting strategies to help them. And to do this we need to connect to other parents and get the emotional support we need.

- ✓ Our children are not able to give us emotional rewards – yet. But with time and support (for us), we see changes.

# 41

# **Sleep**

Parents of children who have suffered trauma often report that trying to get their child settled at night is the most difficult thing – more so because after a day of managing the needs of the children, parents are tired out and need to have a brain break to recharge their batteries even for a couple of hours.

In this chapter, Sarah is getting more and more tired, but the children don't seem to be showing any indication that they are ready to settle at night.

✎ SARAH NAISH: Sleep, please!

*Please go to sleep, I am desperate for rest.*
*It's been a long day and we've all done our best.*
*All I want is some time – to ward off the sorrow,*
*To rest and relax and prepare for tomorrow.*
*Please go to sleep, I know that it's scary.*
*I'll stay here with you, even though you can't bear me.*
*I'll lie down beside you and just close one eye,*
*And when you keep talking I'll try not to sigh.*
*Please go to sleep now, I'll stroke your sweet head,*
*If only you'd actually stay in the bed!*
*I'll read you a story and hear all your fears,*

*I'll sing you a lullaby and wipe up your tears,*
*I'll chase all the monsters, if only you'd let me,*
*I'll hear your sad stories and not show they upset me,*
*I'll do anything, not for me but for you*
*To help you to sleep like happy children do.*

## THE SLEEP MONSTERS (Charley, 9 years; Sophie, 11 years)

*I can't go to sleep*
*Please stay in my room.*
*You walk out the door,*
*Will you be back soon?*
*I can't breathe properly,*
*I want you back NOW.*
*I scream and I cry*
*Or I call you a cow.*
*Why have you left me?*
*Where have you gone?*
*It's been more than five minutes,*
*That's far too long!*
*I start throwing toys*
*And teddies around.*
*What's that in the corner*
*Sat on the ground?*
*The shadows are creepy*
*And I can hear sounds.*
*Has someone come in?*
*Are they creeping about?*
*The horrible thoughts*
*Trapped in my head*
*Get bigger and bigger*

When I come to my bed.
I stare at the light
Through the crack in the door.
Mummy I need you,
I call out some more.
What if they get me
When I fall asleep?
The thoughts in my head
Have moved to my feet.
I jump out of the bed
and rush to the light
I need you right now.
As I move into flight,
You rush up the stairs
And help me to settle.
The noise I can hear
Is only the kettle.
There isn't a monster
Who's got into our home.
You're here to protect me
And I'm not alone.
But I'm still quite scared,
So you sit down to read.
Taking some time to
First name the need,
The need to be near you,
My fear that you've gone,
It's ok to be scared
And I've done nothing wrong.
You hold me and soothe me,
You tell me you care,
We pick up the toys

*And I cuddle my bear.*
*The bad thoughts get smaller*
*And my heart beats less fast.*
*I'm glad you're my mummy*
*Fast asleep at last.*

## WHAT'S HAPPENING HERE?

It's the end of the day. And, like every day, it was a day where Sarah had to be managing multiple complex sets of emotions – her own, her children's and maybe her partner and other family members... It's been hard. We end up, like our children, hypervigilant and stretched to a fine thread. We have been waiting for bedtime and the hope of a little break for our tired brains and bodies. We want to help; we want to understand; heaven knows we want to nurture, but our body is exhausted, our mind is fried. It is so hard to summon up the final resources – sometimes we do not even know if we can.

For the children, the days are scary, but the night is full of nameless terror that lurks under beds and throws shadows on the wall. The children's minds connect easily to their subconscious as they drift off, allowing all their trauma to flood their minds with fear and awful memories. Suddenly they remember that they can never be safe – and maybe for them very bad things happened in the dark. Maybe they had to stay awake to protect themselves or their siblings. Maybe they remember being left alone in their room – with their parents having gone out, who will keep them safe? Sometimes, just as they are dropping off, those horrible thoughts start whizzing around their heads and wake them up again. They had better keep Mum very close, and try to keep awake at all costs!

# ₴ TRY THIS...

✓ Fear is rooted in experience and stress. Help children to feel safe:

- Stay nearby or in the room.

- Have a nightlight.

- Use relaxing aromas like lavender.

- Increase relaxation by giving a hand, foot or head massage.

- Build their trust slowly – explain you need to go and get a cup of tea. Come straight back – prove you are trustworthy. 'I told you I would be back, here I am.'

- Make enough noise to let them know they are not alone. *Consistency, predictability and reliability* build brains – have a routine around bedtime. Stick to it like glue.

- Help the child to move on by giving them a new experience, repeated multiple times. The same bedtime story, the same cuddle, the same mantra – you will keep them safe.

- Don't be in a hurry. Have a book or kindle nearby. Take the opportunity for a cat nap! The more relaxed you are, the more your calm amygdala will calm your child.

# 42

# Honesty

There is a fine balance between telling children the unpalatable truth and protecting them from a history which they are entitled to know. Sometimes, well-meaning professionals or parents can unwittingly sow the seeds of mistrust by attempting to 'silver line' a tragic history.

In Sarah's family there are some difficult truths to be told. How do we approach this and what are the children's views?

## ✎ SARAH NAISH: Questions

The questions seem so innocent and come from nowhere:

'Why didn't Jackie love me?'

'Why did Kevin throw me down the stairs?'

'Why did we get split up for two years?'

My instinct has always told me to be very honest with the children. Their story is one of extreme violence and abuse; children had also died in the birth family. I do not feel able to sugar-coat that. Apart from anything else, Rosie remembers some things that happened. OF COURSE she does!

I find it really hard to listen to others trying to give them a watered-down version. Something along the lines of: 'Jackie and Kevin couldn't look after you properly.' I am sorry, but what does that even MEAN? 'Couldn't look after you properly' infers not having a regular bath, missing a meal, maybe the clothes were a bit ripped and there was shouting and smacking.

How does 'couldn't look after you properly' equate to emotional abuse, calculated cruelty, shoving spoons down a baby's throat to stop them crying? This is *not* a parent who loved the children and was 'doing their best' despite a difficult situation.

No, I will not vilify my children's birth parents. There is a reason for the way they behaved. No doubt they have their own story to tell. But I will not allow my children to take on a single shred of blame or guilt for what happened to them. It was not my children's fault and they deserve to know the truth.

Some of the social workers think I should lie and tell the children that their birth parents loved them as otherwise they will feel bad. I don't agree with that. When I answer their questions honestly and as simply as I can ('Jackie and Kevin could not look after *any* children. You are the best children in the world, and they could not even look after you, Therefore, we know they just weren't up to it.'), I can SEE the relief on the children's faces. They know the truth already. I will not collude in society's lie. They must be able to trust at least one person.

BUT... Oh my goodness, some of those truths were hard to tell. They serrated my heart as I told them. With every truth, I could see the pieces of the puzzle falling into place. Yes, it was sad, dreadful, painful scary, terrifying. No, it should never have happened. No, you should never have been left there. But it *did* happen and I will never ever let it happen again.

## ⌘ SO MANY WHYS (All children, any age)

Why did the social workers lie to us, lie to me? They said they were moving us as, although Jackie and Kevin loved us, they couldn't look after us properly.

They said we needed to be kept safe. Kept safe! What an absolute joke that was. There were so many times they came to the house and could see we weren't safe but they didn't do anything! I tried to tell them we were in danger. I tried to tell them with my eyes. Maybe they didn't care.

I had so many whys.

I felt like a really bad person.

If they loved us, why weren't we good enough to be looked after properly? Why did they hurt us, not feed us properly?

Why was I so frightened of the people who I was told loved me?

It made no sense at all.

If that was love, I wanted nothing to do with it. Love hurt.

Eventually, I started to feel safer and began to believe that maybe we weren't going back, that Mummy was keeping us forever.

I asked Mummy all of these questions. She helped me to understand. She told me the TRUTH!

All I ever wanted was the truth. I could see it was hard for her to tell me, but it was the most helpful thing she could ever have done.

The truth was ugly but it was the truth.

I started to realise that Kevin and Jackie didn't love me – not because I'm a bad person but because they can't love anyone. They don't know what love is.

I am now learning what real love is.

Thank you, Mummy.

Thank you for the truth. X

## WHAT'S HAPPENING HERE?

In Sarah's children's birth family there were high levels of abuse, cruelty and violence. It is not possible to reconcile that with the fairy tale of 'being loved'. It is important to reiterate that in this chapter we are not talking about those families where there is genine reciprocal love but other factors have contributed to the children being in care. Whatever the situation, honesty is the answer.

Parents often give us different scenarios at training when we speak about this:

'Ah, but what about the fact that my child's birth mother has gone on to have further children who live at home?'

'Ah, but what about the fact that the birth father killed the birth mother?'

The answer is always the same: 'Be honest!'

In this chapter, we can feel the anger, frustration and relief of the mother and the confusion of the child, which then changes to gratitude as their story is related truthfully, allowing them to start the terrible process of accommodating that knowledge – grieving, reacting and then healing.

Too often in handing over information, language is used which is designed to protect the child's feelings, but this just ends up being patronising and inaccurate. Every aspect is downplayed or re-imagined by using language which simply avoids the facts. The reason for this may be fear that no one will take on the child, or it may be protective of the child. It may be that the teller cannot accept or imagine the experiences the child had. It might be a 'nicer truth' for them!

Unfortunately, all that happens is that having been given a totally erroneous impression of what our children lived through, we have more difficulty understanding behaviours and reactions. If we have a true picture, we can be more effective, more empathic. It is, of course, incredibly hard, but it is also incredibly hard to try to help children recover from trauma without all the facts, and massively confusing and scary for children to hear their watered-down stories, which throw doubt on their memories and perception, or make them feel that everything they endured is a secret and no one knows. The children may think, 'They will not believe me. I didn't take enough care. I was bad.'

## ♟ REMEMBER...

✓ We do not protect children from their experiences by ignoring them or sugar-coating them. The children were there – witnesses and victims of the unspeakable. If we are not brave enough to validate them with truth, we cannot truly connect and empathise. The children may feel they need to protect us from the truth which will drive feelings of isolation and disconnect for them.

✓ We should not collude in the worst lie of all – that their parents loved them. This is a statement designed to protect the abusers, not the child. How can we expect a child to accept love, if they associate this with terror, hunger and pain? Is it right to ask them to call us Mum or Dad, if we do not explain to them that we know the difference?

✓ You will notice that in this family the mum refers to birth parents by their first names, which allows the title of Mum or Dad to have new significance.

✓ Don't collude with half-truths which breed mistrust. Tell children the truth.

## ✎ SARAH NAISH: A new relationship

Having been a single parent for a number of years with all the challenges we faced, I had written off any hope of having a relationship. I was astonished, therefore, when I met Ray, who seemed quite normal *and* did not run a mile!

I was lucky that he was also a parent, but of course parenting securely attached children is entirely different from parenting traumatised children.

The children were still young when we met. Charley was 8 years old, Sophie 10, William 11, Katie 12, and Rosie 14.

I was very wary about introducing Ray to the children as I did not want them to have to try to get to know a new person in their life, who then might disappear! I was also aware that Ray would need to embark on a vertical learning curve about a new way of parenting.

In due course, when I realised that Ray was a pretty exceptional person (and 'a keeper'), I gradually introduced him to the children.

After a year he moved in with us and became a central figure within the family.

# 43

# Avoiding Connection

It is common for traumatised children to resist re-attaching to a safe adult. How can they be sure that this person will not let them down? This is not a 'choice' but a fear-driven, self-protective mechanism and can be very difficult to overcome.

Even though the children have been with Sarah for eight years, one of the main challenges she is facing here is trying to connect to her children when they will not accept that connection.

✎ SARAH NAISH: Closed

I have always known that Sophie was 'the hand grenade child', the one who skilfully deflects attention from herself to ensure we are focusing on the others.

With Ray joining the family I have had to work hard to help him see that what is on the surface is not a true reflection of her. Naturally, we have entered a new phase where she is busy reinventing herself for Ray's benefit! Lots of charming and fake smiles.

I wonder what is happening behind Sophie's eyes? As she turns her face to gaze steadfastly away from me, I can see she is only looking within. She always says she's 'just fine' and everything is 'OK'. I wonder, should I push her more, or just step back and wait?

It's like a physical barrier between us. Sometimes she manages to create an actual barrier though. This might be being very 'busy' or suddenly having to urgently find a 'lost thing'.

She avoids intimacy at all costs. It doesn't matter how light-hearted or fun I try to make it. Her wary eyes are always one step ahead. Watching, waiting.

This child is the one who is furthest away from my longest reach. The closer I move to her, the more swiftly she moves away.

She is the child that school say is 'no problem' and is 'so good'. They don't seem to be able to see her huge well of sadness. They don't realise that everything she does is to protect herself, to avoid sharing herself or making a connection.

I know what she likes to eat (mostly beige food). I know that her friends like her but don't seem to really know her either. I know that she works hard to make sure my focus stays on the other children so that she stays invisible. Sometimes she does this by throwing a hand grenade and standing back while the 'victim' acts out, getting the audience.

I don't know her favourite colour, her best toy, what makes her happy, what makes her sad. I can't know because she cannot make choices that reveal anything about her.

My sad, stuck, disconnected little girl. How on earth can I help her?


## POSSUM CHILD (Sophie, 12 years)

*I am a possum child,*
*You might just think I'm dead,*
*Shutting out the world,*
*Hiding in my head.*

*I am a possum child,*
*Closed down and reserved.*
*I only nod or grunt,*
*I act like I've not heard.*

*I am a possum child,*
*I always like to sleep,*
*I stay up in my room,*
*Until it's time to eat.*

*I am a possum child,*
*Everything is fine,*
*I have an awful memory,*
*I cannot tell the time.*

*I am a possum child,*
*Compliant all the while,*
*Dead inside my eyes,*
*Faking every smile.*

*I am a possum child,*
*Going with the flow,*
*Underneath the radar,*
*So no one ever knows.*

*I am a possum child,*
*Deep within my soul*
*Burns a scary fire,*
*My anger is the coal.*

*I am a possum child,*
*If someone gets too close,*
*I back off in my cave,*
*Glad to be morose.*

*I am a possum child,*
*I'm just about alive,*
*I stay here in the shadows,*
*It's how I must survive.*

*I am a possum child,*
*Lonely to the core,*
*I rarely show emotion*
*But gaze towards the floor.*

*I am a possum child,*
*I know it drives you crazy,*
*You think that I'm not bothered,*
*You say that I am lazy.*

*I am a possum child,*
*I cannot bear your touch,*
*And when you say you care,*
*I find it all too much.*

*I am a possum child,*
*My body feels too numb*
*I wish that I could trust you,*
*I wish I felt you're Mum.*

*I am a possum child,*
*But please don't leave me be,*
*I really need to be here,*
*Yet I'm scared of company.*

*I am a possum child,*
*So please approach softly,*
*Although I need you close by,*
*I cannot bear you near me.*

*I am a possum child,*
*But I'm desperate to belong,*
*I'd like to get to know you,*
*But I'm scared I'll get it wrong.*

*I am a possum child,*
*I hope you understand,*
*It might just take me ages,*
*But I'd like to hold your hand.*

*I am a possum child,*
*As slowly you draw near,*
*I feel my body warming,*
*Thawing out the fear.*

*I am a possum child,*
*So please do take things slow,*
*I'd like to try to trust you,*
*But trust takes time to grow.*

*I am a possum child,*
*But hiding deep within,*
*Is a lovely girl,*
*Who wants to let you in.*

## WHAT'S HAPPENING HERE?

Sometimes the past experiences are so hard to bear that Sophie takes steps to protect herself from more pain. It all happened so long ago, when she was so young – all she knows is that she cannot afford to be vulnerable, to trust, to love. Those are things that bring pain. As we all seek affection, Sophie might need a pet – a dog, a guinea pig – that will love her, ask no tricky questions, and make no demands. Not being human, pets receive and give affection with no judgement, and no strings attached.

With Sophie, it is so much a part of her psychology to be afraid and to mistrust; she protects herself by shutting herself away. Changing this is immensely hard. The armour is in place, not a chink anywhere.

Now, with Ray joining the family, Sophie is working extra hard to ensure she is safe and that no one gets to see 'the real her'. This would be very risky.

## ♟ REMEMBER...

- ✓ We are hardwired to be social. The child's subconscious in this case is in turmoil, seeking comfort but scared that it will bring pain.

- ✓ The brain is a very plastic organ. We can help to change the way the child perceives us, and from there the world (just like when they learned to self-protect as a baby).

- ✓ We need to be gentle, to be present (but not pushy), to meet needs quietly, knowing that the child knows who left their lunch out, but not requiring a response.

- ✓ We need to be *consistent*, *predictable and reliable* in our support, and let the child know that we understand why they cannot let us in; but here we are, nonetheless, watching and waiting and loving them.

# 44

# Who Cares?

One of the hardest challenges therapeutic parents face is the apparent lack of empathy from their children. In the face of any of life's difficult moments, from illness to bereavement, these can be made even worse by the apparent self-centredness of the children.

Sarah seems to struggle with the effects of the children's lack of empathy. She is expecting empathy, or at least hoping for some, but the children are not on the same page...at all! This becomes even more serious when Sarah's father dies.

## ✎ SARAH NAISH: Ill

I feel so ill. This morning I could hardly get out of bed. I don't know what I would do if Ray wasn't here.

I have come down with the same thing that Sophie has had. I know it was really stupid to hope that someone might help me – of course, that was a forlorn hope. I told Charley I felt ill (she is the only one who seems OK) but all she cared about was if her tea would be on time! I swear the children only care about themselves and don't even notice what is going on around them. I have tried explaining how I feel, but they just look at me like I am speaking a different language.

At present they are having a 'who is the illest' competition with each other. I don't count, obviously.

To be honest, it's probably best if I just keep going with the painkillers and try to act normal. If they sense any sign of weakness, they seem to up the ante. The more ill or tired I feel, the more they play up. It's like having a room full of toddlers!

Last week, Charley's friend, Amy, came into school so upset because her guinea pig had died. Apparently Charley said, 'Oh well it was only a guinea pig.' She then asked what Amy had in her sandwich box. I think that was because Amy had said she was too upset to eat. When the teacher challenged Charley, she didn't seem to understand what the issue was. The teacher told her to say sorry, but Charley just looked at her blankly.

Am I raising a child with no empathy whatsoever?

## ✎ SARAH NAISH: Losing Dad

I lost my dad. He died at Christmas. I am devastated, heartbroken. He was my rock. My one strong truth in this mad world. I cannot deal with the children. I cannot look at their pain of losing Granddad. Maybe they don't care. They seem more focused on where their next meal is coming from. I don't think I can cope with this. They have known him for ten years and he loved them. He was Granddad. They just seem to want to check that I am still going to be able to carry on as normal. Their behaviours are worse. More fighting. More arguing. Let me out please!

I am so thankful that Ray joined our family a year ago. He has been literally a godsend in this situation. He placed himself in the 'front line', dealing empathically with the children's grief and giving them all the necessary explanations. He also fielded some of the more unkind questions. I know this means I am more alone with my grief, but at least there is a sense of peace there.

## ⋈ I DON'T CARE (Charley, 10 years)

Today has been a very horrible day. The dog had to go to the vet's. It's not fair as we were meant to be going to the new soft play centre in town and now we can't go. Stupid dog!

Also, Rosie has a very bad cold, Sophie is very hot and Mummy doesn't feel well either.

What am I going to do? There will be no one to play with me! William and Katie seem to be OK, but I'm not friends with them at the moment. They wouldn't let me have their sweets. They are very nasty to me!

At least Mummy is still cooking the dinner, so that's OK. I hope she hurries up.

Sophie is getting a lot of attention from Mummy. Mummy thinks that Sophie is in pain and maybe has a virus. What's a virus? She has checked her temperature more times than she's ever checked mine. Maybe I should say I'm hot too. Rosie keeps sneezing and it's very annoying when you're trying to watch the telly. I hope Mummy soon tells her to stop as she's not listening to me at all.

It's like when Amy said her guinea pig had died. It was only a flipping guinea pig! All I did was laugh and ask if she still wanted her lunch, but Mummy said I need to think about how other people are feeling and learn to be kind. I don't care how they feel. Why should I? Mummy said I needed to say sorry for asking for her lunch. I said I would say sorry but I'm not really sorry. I just want Mummy to shut up so she can finish the dinner. Maybe Ray will take me out for a treat to make up for my horrible day?

This has all been very boring and I'm fed up with always getting blamed when I've done nothing wrong. I always get blamed for everything

Shut up everyone and just bring me my tea!

## ⛬ SORRY...NOT SORRY (William, 13 years)

*I am not sorry,*
*I don't care what you say,*
*I wish you would shut up,*
*I wish you'd go away.*

*Sitting in my bedroom,*
*Giving me the talk,*
*I want to get a drink now,*
*So I get up and walk.*

*Shouting from the bedroom*
*For me to come right back,*
*I zone you out my head*
*I'm very good at that.*

*You are very angry now*
*That I will not say sorry,*
*So I say it very quickly,*
*Then I can get that lolly.*

*Why am I uncaring?*
*You've asked me very often,*
*So I say that I care,*
*And that makes your heart soften.*

*Sadly though it doesn't last,*
*I'm back to my old tricks.*
*You think that I am bad*
*And I'm doing it for kicks.*

*So you've written out some rules*
*That we must all obey.*
*I agree to keep them,*
*Then run back out to play.*

## ꩜ LOSING GRANDDAD (Charley, 10 years)

Oh well, that's just great, isn't it? Granddad has died now and I am VERY sad. I have done lots of sad faces to show everyone how sad I actually am.

I don't know where he has gone. Where do dead people go? I keep asking Mummy, but she just keeps crying. I expect this means my tea will be late. Everything feels very wobbly. Mummy seems to have forgotten about me. Yes, it is sad about Granddad, of course, but if Mummy forgets to feed us I might actually die too. Will I see Granddad in heaven then? Maybe I could suggest that to Mummy? I could take a message. That might even cheer her up a bit.

Ray says that's probably not a good idea. Fine then.

## WHAT'S HAPPENING HERE? ▬▬▬▬▬▬

### Empathy

First of all, it is really important to remember that empathy and feeling appropriate guilt (so that you can say sorry) are not things that happen on their own. They are learned from the modelling of the people around you. Children observe behaviour and learn from it all the time. They are like little sponges absorbing their family's ways of caring and behaving. Saying sorry (and meaning it) happens when we recognise that our 'naughty' actions are separate from us (around the ages of 2–4 years with good enough parenting). Empathy occurs with repetition as we experience empathy from our parents, and feel the comfort this brings, and then express this to others.

The children's viewpoints, reflected here by William and Charley are interesting because they had different early life experiences. Empathy is not yet present with Charley due to pre-natal stress and high cortisol levels. That, and growing up with four siblings who are not demonstrating empathy! William and other children who come into families for adoption, fostering or kinship care, or those who suffer an early life disruption due to illness or other circumstances, have not had this experience. In fact, their existence has depended on their ability to survive. Survival is at its most basic a solitary and 'selfish' need. Other people (siblings, for example) may be a threat to survival if there is only a little bit to go round (like food, for example). You cannot afford to be empathic if it will affect your survival chances.

**Bereavement**

When a parent of a traumatised child suffers a close family bereavement, this can be one of the biggest challenges. Here Sarah is devastated by the loss of her father but she knows she cannot look to the children for any kind of support. Charley is feeling very worried about the changes in her mum. She is unable to access real empathy but knows what it should look like by now. She can only interpret events by what they mean to *her*.

This is not her fault. Is Mum going to die now? Is she still safe? Will Mum forget about her? The only way she can work this out is to test it. This means testing Mum. Poor Sarah. Poor Charley.

## ♀ REMEMBER...

- ✓ To express sorry and mean it, and to express empathy, require activation of a specific area of the brain, first developing and then strengthening those neurological synapses.

- ✓ This can only be achieved when the person understands and perceives that their physiological (food, air, water), safety (no drunk/abusive/violent parent in the house) and belonging (phew! I feel safe and comfortable with this parent) needs are met.

✓ However, the optimal initial time for brain development and 'hardwiring' your responses to survive is very early on – up to 18 months – and depends on an attuned parent to meet your survival, safety and love needs. After that, it happens, but it takes time, many repetitions, much role modelling, relationship repairs and practice. And it's hard. Just remember – consistency, predictability and reliability build brains and this takes a LONG time!

✓ If you suffer a close bereavement or significant negative life event, it's a good idea to put someone else in the front line, as Sarah did here with Ray, to deal with the children's expression of grief and difficult questions about the distressing event. This enables you to grieve and process your own loss.

✓ Take a brain break – a mindful moment – yourself to give you the strength and stamina to carry on.

# 45

# **Stealing**

Stealing (or taking things) happens very frequently, and often at an unconscious level. Stealing might have helped the children to survive in the past but it can be very difficult for parents to accept once the trauma is in the past and there appears to be no 'need' for the child to steal.

With five children to look after, four of them having experienced deprivation, things were bound to go missing. With so many children it's even harder to work out who took it. The scale and frequency of the stealing is getting Sarah and Ray down.

✎ SARAH NAISH: Thieves

It started off with food. There was no way I could leave anything sweet lying about, or even put away or hidden. It's like my children have super senses and can sniff anything out!

It's much harder with money. I can't leave anything lying around; everything has to be locked away. When friends come to the house, I put their handbags in my room and lock it. It's very embarrassing. I have taken to wearing a bum-bag all the time. It contains my credit cards, keys, phone and money. This has given me some peace of mind.

William is the main culprit, although all the children have stolen money at some point. Three of them have also indulged in a bit of shoplifting. It's so draining. A lot of blame came my way. I should be 'supervising them better' or we 'don't have strict enough boundaries'! It's ridiculous. People assume that this stealing is on the same level as the teenager taking the odd fiver out of a purse. IT'S NOT! It is relentless and exhausting.

William will leave the house as if he's going to see friends. Then when I go out, he will break back in. He has caused lots of damage breaking back in. That's more hassle than the actual stealing. I think Ray is getting fed up with fixing the doors all the time!

William doesn't care about the effect it has on me and he steals quite blatantly. He is no good at hiding the money, so he tends to spend it straightaway. I have a safe now and this means he can't steal anything, but it doesn't stop him trying!

None of the children NEED to steal anything. They have everything they want. Other people don't think so though. If they are caught stealing, they are very good at convincing shopkeepers/police that they were hungry/had no shoes, etc.! I have actually had the police here checking William had shoes after he told them a sob story when he was caught shoplifting. Why don't others get it? If they supported me and realised what was happening, we could stop this. I feel so helpless.

## ❧ THIEF (Charley, 10 years; William, 13 years)

*I've got a terrible feeling in my chest.*
*It's like a bird that won't take a rest.*
*I'm struggling to breathe and I feel really sick,*
*My head feels heavy and my heart like a brick.*

*I don't want to take things but they say I'm a thief,*
*I'll be in prison if I keep on like this.*
*I must be as bad as I think I am,*
*Disgusting, unlovable, totally mad!*

*When I steal stuff, I get a great big high.*
*It makes all the bad feelings appear to die.*
*Not for long though as it's worse when I'm done.*
*I know I'm not worthy of being your son.*

*Like a scratch that I've got to itch, an urge that I can't control,*
*For a moment, a second, it makes me feel whole.*
*I forget about everything else at the time,*
*I just want it, I have it, even though it's not mine.*

*I will take things I don't even need and sometimes I throw*
    *them away.*
*I lie and say 'it wasn't me' or find someone else to blame.*
*At night I lay awake as waves of shame envelop my soul.*
*To be a thief was never my goal.*

*Like a self-harmer who cuts their arm,*
*A warm whooshy feeling and then some calm.*
*A break from the bird that's trapped in their chest,*
*Unable to verbalise their internal mess.*

*It's like driving a car without any brakes.*
*A liar, a thief, he steals, he takes.*
*My brain doesn't tell me to STOP, it's not mine!*
*That part of my brain just isn't online.*

I can't stop stealing, I don't want to take things and I feel like a criminal afterwards.

When I get caught, I always promise it won't happen again, but it does even though I don't mean for it to happen. I've got stuff hidden under my bed, in my sock drawer and even behind the bush in the garden, but thinking about it makes me feel disgusting. I feel sick and can't even bear to look at the things I've taken.

I wish someone would help me to stop. I don't want to get into trouble, but strangely enough, I actually feel relieved once I've been found out.

## WHAT'S HAPPENING HERE?

You can really feel the sense of frustration and helplessness that Sarah experiences in this situation – and for many parents this is compounded and made more complex by the feelings of guilt and shame that they experience for their children's behaviour; their apprehension of how this reflects on their ability to parent; and their fear for the children, their present experience and their futures. The isolation is terrible because the explanations are so hard and shaming, and the judgement and blame that follow discourage parents from seeking support. There is a sense of being a prisoner in your own home – having to lock things away. It just feels so wrong. Damage to property, breaking in, a real sense of violation of your home and of your feelings – a betrayal of all you are giving. In addition to this is the overriding question – WHY?

Firstly, we can see a mirror of the adult's feelings in the child – shame, isolation, judgement, blame and violation. This is really apparent. In addition, there is an appallingly low self-esteem, a feeling of 'wrongness', of 'badness' and there is a pervasive quality to this – in other words, these feelings are felt within the child, as part of the child, *not* as a response to the action of stealing. William describes the terrible feelings of fearfulness and anxiety in his chest – a horrible fluttering that won't subside. How can he help himself? Another child would turn to an adult. But he cannot do this – adults bring pain, shame and rejection. He has never experienced the comfort of an attuned adult or been supported to manage his huge feelings of disappointment, fear or rage: instead, he has learned to substitute food and 'things' for the comfort he craves. At least there is a brief relief from the stress and pressure of feeling so bad all the time. If you asked him why he steals, he would not be able to give you a proper answer. He might say, 'I felt like it,' but this is because he has no insight into his huge pain and losses. He throws things away because they do not get to the root of the issue: the toxic shame that makes him believe that if you asked what the problem is, he might say, 'Me. I'm the problem. It's all my fault. It's *always* my fault.'

## ℞ TRY THIS...

✓ We need to accept children as they are. They need support to overcome shame while you are helping them to learn about relationships, trust and connection. So, try the following:

- Think about their history. I remember a child who was taught to steal, and punished if they were caught.

- Think about their emotional pain. Use empathy – it's hard to ask for help if you have never had it.

- It may feel impossible for them to trust. Show that you are trustworthy, and they will learn that they are worthwhile.

- Remove temptation – it feels horrible to lock things away, as Sarah describes very well, but this way you create a way for the child to succeed.

- Be *consistent, predictable and reliable*. Help them to activate those areas of the brain that have never been used and to form new ideas about themselves, the family, and the world. Show them they are not alone.

– Use natural consequences to help them develop their impulse control, and be understanding and patient when this is hard. Help them to manage and give names to their feelings and their needs.

As always, this is a process. It takes time, love, patience and commitment. Your child may never be completely free of the impulses arising from trauma, but with your help and support they will learn to recognise and manage them.

## A FINAL INSIGHT

We can offer a unique perspective into the difficulties and the deeply ingrained nature of these impulses, as well as the tenacity of the negative thoughts which are never far from the surface, in these words which are the adult reflection of a child from care.

### ⌘ HELP ME (WILLIAM)

*I need you to help me to calm the bird,*
*To listen, to hold me and tell me you've heard,*
*To find ways to comfort my aching heart and*
*Lessen the pain that tears me apart.*

*Please can you gently rewire my brain*
*And find ways to reduce my toxic shame,*
*To reassure me and let me know*
*You're not giving up and you're not letting go.*

*Remove the temptation and come alongside,*
*Name the need that chooses to hide.*
*Show me ways to put things right,*
*To link cause and effect without a fight.*

*And as I begin to grow my brain,*
*You will eventually see a change,*
*A beautiful lovely boy underneath,*
*No longer unworthy, no longer a THIEF.*

# 46

# Rudeness

When therapeutic parents are asked what they find most challenging of all, rudeness is absolutely guaranteed to be near the top of the list (sometimes described as disrespect, defiance, etc.). This behaviour might be shown through swearing, arguing, insulting the parent or simply ignoring direct instruction.

In this chapter, there seems to be an underlying constant current of rudeness, which Sarah is really struggling with. What is that all about?

### ✎ SARAH NAISH: The rude girls

The rudeness from Rosie and Charley is quite intolerable at times. It seems to seep from their mouths all the way through their bodies. It's in gestures, eye rolling, dismissing me and others, stomping up and down the stairs, slamming doors, sighing and huffing loudly. Or it can be generally ungrateful, not sorry for anything, and expecting everything as their right!

When people see this, they just think I'm a bad parent. Maybe I am? I just know that if I rise to it, it makes things 100 times worse. I do hold my boundaries and I'm very clear about what I will and will not accept. But sometimes it is honestly easier to pretend I haven't seen something rather than to start again with the whole 'That's not OK. You need to apologise, etc.'

I think the worst thing is the way they dismiss me so easily when I'm trying to help them. It's so embarrassing when they do this in front of my own parents or friends and relatives. Generally speaking, the children aren't so rude when we are at home alone, but when I have an audience that's when it starts. It's anything from low-level sniping to attempts to embarrass me or get a reaction from me. I work really hard to stay stable and give them a muted response, making sure that they know I know and will be taking action. I suppose it has almost become a theme tune to our life. Just background noises of rudeness to each other, to me, to Ray.

I do wonder how they will ever manage when they leave school and go to work. I can't imagine that anyone will employ them or put up with being answered back to, with the insistence that they are always right and everyone else is an idiot!

Oh, the joys to come.

## I AM RUDE (Charley, 10 years)

I am rude because my brother and sisters speak to me or each other that way and I'm used to it.

I am rude because I like the feeling of power and control it gives me, especially as I often feel very out of control on the inside.

I am rude because it gives me an outlet for all my pent-up emotions that I struggle to identify.

I am rude because it gets me attention, even if it's negative attention.

I am rude because I know it winds you up and I like to be in control of you.

I am rude because I can't think before I behave in a certain way or say the wrong thing.

I am rude because I can't help it.

## 💬 I AM RUDE (Rosie, 16 years)

I am rude because people in my past spoke to me or each other that way and I'm used to it.

I am rude because I know it winds you up and I like to be in control of you, so I don't feel as scared.

I am rude because I'm tired, hungry, thirsty or just want a cuddle but don't realise I'm feeling these things.

I am rude because I push you away and reject you before you reject me!

I am rude because I want to elicit the same response from you that I received in my previous/birth family. It feels comfortable when you behave in a way I expect, even though it's not good for me and just proves I'm right and that all adults are the same.

I am rude because you've done something nice with me or for me and I want to remind you that I'm a bad kid. I don't believe I deserve good/nice things so I sabotage everything.

I am rude because you got too close and I'm scared of attachment.

I am rude because that's the label I've been given by everyone, so I might as well live up to it.

I am mostly rude because I'm scared!

## WHAT'S HAPPENING HERE?

It is really tough for parents to tolerate rudeness. Rude equals 'nasty', 'bad mannered', 'badly brought up'. These perceptions are playing on Mum's deepest fear as a parent – that she is not actually up to the job, not good enough.

An additional factor underlies this perception – our own childhood experience. We cannot help it; our subconscious activates old scripts that our parents used. We are easily activated by the same triggers. And we struggle so much to find reasons that are rational.

But we can't find any. We end up feeling 'I don't deserve this' or even 'I did not sign up for this, I can't manage'.

The first and strongest parenting model is a child's own parents. Here we have two slightly different feelings around needing to 'be rude': Rosie's drivers are fear-based; but as Charley had all her early needs met, her drivers are quite different!

Rosie describes how children are triggered easily into a defensive stance – one of distrust and disbelief. Kindness, comfort and being cared for feel very uncomfortable. It is better to act out the behaviour that confirms their own feelings and beliefs ('I don't deserve this'). Thus parent and child have mirror emotions: one from a fear of inadequacy; the other from toxic shame and anxiety.

Vulnerability induces fear. When a child feels themselves opening up to feelings of safety and security, it causes stress. When you start relaxing, that is when you are in most danger. It is much worse when there is an audience there, of course (more adults to keep an eye on) causing the child to lash out verbally or act out. But how or when were these children shown respect? What was the language of their life? Were small treats and kindnesses the prelude to unspeakable acts? Their systems are saying, 'You can't fool me. I know you are the same as the others. You are just taking longer to show your true colours. But I can and will control this situation!'

Some children have been removed at birth and been with foster parents from the word 'go'. So, they should be OK? Well, no. The separation from the birth mum, the in-utero trauma, the stress levels of Mum, and the genetic heritage all play a part affecting levels of cortisol and therefore the ability to manage stress and respond in a socially appropriate way.

## ☀ THINK...

- ✓ Consider this: If we choose to ignore certain behaviours, we can take control of the situation and our responses. This is not letting the children 'get away with it'; it is a deliberate strategy to reduce stress and conflict and increase connection. It means we understand the underlying issues. We will continue to reflect on behaviours and provide appropriate models.

- ✓ Keep in mind that stress induces opposition and defiance. Ignore the defiance, keep control. Give the child time to process and respond appropriately.

## ✒ TRY THIS...

- ✓ Pause... Keep your own brain connected. Your calm amygdala (the 'fire alarm' of the brain, detecting danger) has the ability to calm your child's amygdala.

- ✓ Time, patience and practice will win the day.

# 47

# **Grief**

Underpinning challenging behaviours is incredible heartbreak for both parent and child. Here we see a glimpse of those raw feelings which are rarely acknowledged.

✎ SARAH NAISH: Why weren't you born to me?

*Why weren't you born to me? Child of my heart,*
*Why did you have to endure such pain at the start?*
*Why weren't you born to me? The child I longed to hold,*
*We could have built magical memories,*
*Warmth instead of cold.*
*It grieves my heart to look at you*
*And feel the fear you knew,*
*Because had you been born to me*
*I would have died to save you.*

⭕ WHY WASN'T I BORN TO YOU? (Any
   of the children, 16+ years)

*Mother of my dreams,*
*Why was I unloved?*
*I wish I'd been born to you,*
*Grown inside your belly,*

*Comforted by your voice,*
*Rocked and soothed.*
*Would you have loved me more?*
*I know you would have protected me,*
*Saved me from my terror,*
*Like a lion with her cubs.*
*I see the sadness in your eyes,*
*For you could not be there.*
*I want to see myself reflected in your gaze.*
*I feel the bond between our hearts.*
*I know I am loved*
*But I missed you at the start.*
*I missed you so much,*
*Mother of my dreams*

## WHAT'S HAPPENING HERE?

For parents, grief is revisited time and time again. For some, there is the grief they feel for their unborn children. For what should have been. This can be tinged with anger at the unfairness of a world where pregnancy comes easily to mums who do not take care – ignoring their pregnancy and the needs of their unborn child and continuing toxic lifestyles. Grief is revisited in our growing understanding of our children, the obstacles they face. The loss of the dream we had of a 'perfect family', or of future hopes and dreams. Sometimes we have grief due to isolation, the distancing that occurs from friends, and even family, who fail to understand the challenging behaviours. We grieve for our children, who suffer and still wonder why they were so bad that they were abandoned, used, and finally rejected. Sometimes grief can be overwhelming and unexpected, triggered by a lyric, or a film, or a memory. We strive to find a balance, because grief can plunge us into despair or compassion fatigue, and we learn to celebrate and build our future hopes on small achievements and gestures of love from our children.

Children grieve for their lost families. They wish they were the same as everyone else. For them, grief is pervasive and links with shame and feelings of responsibility for things that were done to them or their siblings.

As they connect to us gradually and painfully, our children grieve because they were not born into the family. They cannot understand, sometimes asking mums why they did not let them be born in their tummies. It's like a grief that they were born to be different. Words do not seem to relieve that ache, but empathy, love and patience can be transforming over time.

## ♀ REMEMBER...

- ✓ Our own experience of grief gives us empathy to understand and to console our child. We are mirrors of each other's experience. Out of this grief we can grow and heal together.

# 48

# Moving On

As children grow through the teenage years, there is a biological need to seek independence. It is natural and common for children who have suffered trauma, and perhaps lived in fear for the early part of their lives, to seek independence as a means to feeling in control of their lives. Sadly, this often does not work out as we all hope due to the mismatch between their emotional and chronological age.

In this chapter, stress levels are rising in the family as the children start to push for independence in different ways. This is a pivotal time in the family.

## ✎ SARAH NAISH: Letting go, not giving up

As the children are becoming more independent they seem to think they are officially grown up!

### Rosie

Rosie in particular could not wait to leave home! At 16 she was very keen to leave and prove that she could go it alone. She had very limited funds but was determined to break free from her 'annoying' family.

With a heavy heart I helped her to move into bedsit accommodation, which was all she could afford. I felt like I had failed. Strangely enough, one of our first really connected moments was when I had to leave her and we both held on to each other and cried.

I expected Rosie to be home within a few days but I had underestimated her sheer determination to forge a life for herself.

I cannot pretend that it was not quieter and less stressful at home though! There was much less fighting between the younger children. I was worried they would miss her, but they just seemed to merge together to fill the gap.

I kept in touch by text and phone and made sure Rosie had food. I didn't give her any money but I did show her how to do 'budget shopping'. She did not like that very much.

After three months we had a late-night SOS call to say that some nasty people had 'had a party' in her bedsit. She did not know what to do and had clearly been very scared. Ray and I went round to help her clear up and to put some strategies in place. We took her out for lunch and I could almost feel a seismic shift within her...towards me! This felt like progress.

It was so tempting to ask her to come back home, but I knew we had to hold our nerve and wait.

Over the next three months we saw each other more, engaged on a more meaningful level and made a new deal. Rosie would move back home and live semi-independently.

I did not expect this to work, to be honest, but the difference in Rosie on her return was startling.

Gone was the moody belligerent teenager and in her place was a much more well-rounded young woman who suddenly seemed to have maturity, empathy and insight. I had no idea how it happened, but this was the beginning for our new relationship – the relationship I had always wanted with my daughter. Friendship, mutual respect and laughter!

**William**

William left home at 18. Initially he rejected everyone and moved in with a family who did not know his background or his trauma. He reinvented himself. Yes, that is painful, but I know my son has some very good foundations now and he will get there. We all have to work through our own stuff in our own way. We stay in touch and, little by little, are moving back closer together. The important thing with him is to keep those lines of communication open, avoid blame and just keep trying in a low-level way. I will never give up on him but I have learned to let him go… Because that is what HE needs for now.

## LEAVING (Rosie, 16–17 years)

I was so fed up with living at home. Mummy got on my nerves, trying to boss me around, treating me like a 2-year-old! I wanted my own place – I was 16 years old, for crying out loud.

I'd always managed to take care of myself, so what could possibly go wrong? I'd have £30 per week education allowance so I'd be just fine. I didn't shut up about it and made life very difficult for everyone at home. Eventually, she gave in and allowed me to leave.

It wasn't easy when Mummy and Ray dropped me off at the bedsit, and I found it hard to let her go when she hugged me goodbye, but I didn't crumble. I was bigger than that, or so I thought. I stuck my tough shell back on!

The first few weeks were great. I could come and go as I pleased, have all my friends over to visit, stay up for as long as I wanted. Yet inside I felt lonely. I looked forward to Mummy dropping some food round. I regularly checked my phone for her text.

I didn't let her know though. I was sure she thought I was perfectly fine and I didn't want her doing her 'told you so' face!

I didn't think she missed me. Why would she?

It all got a bit scary after a party at my place. People turned up who I hadn't invited. They wouldn't leave. I wanted my mummy. I even wanted Ray. I called them but only because it was an emergency. They helped me to clean up and sort out a plan to avoid it happening again. It felt like they really cared.

I missed living with them. I missed the safety of home, the routine and even the stupid rules. Mummy and I met up quite regularly after that. I actually enjoyed her company! I began to look at her differently, to trust her even. It was like I'd grown up all of a sudden and realised where I was and what I needed. I needed my mummy, I needed my family. I even needed Ray! For a man, he actually isn't too bad. He does do what he says he will and he never huffs and sighs. He mended my phone for me so I could still text. I think he is like a dad is supposed to be.

## LEAVE ME ALONE (William, 16 years)

*Being a teen is sodding hard work, I'm always accused of being a jerk.*

*They say that I'm grumpy, selfish bad, No one takes time to realise I'm sad.*

*You see that I'm growing, yet inside I'm small. I cannot 'behave' so I'm kicked out of school.*

*I'm constantly told that I must act my age, but I am still stuck at the toddler stage!*

*My early life needs are remaining unmet. All I can see is the world is a threat,*

*A threat to my safety and need to survive. I find it far better to stay here and hide.*

*I hide in my bedroom out of the way, living in games for most of the day.*

*Virtual reality is now my new home, or spending six hours*
*glued to my phone.*
*I want to avoid this growing up bit, but everyone thinks I'm*
*an ignorant git.*
*I pull up my hoodie when I venture downstairs, to block out*
*the noise of your tutting and glares.*
*If only you knew how I truly am feeling, the pain in my heart*
*would leave you all reeling.*
*Reeling with guilt that you wish you had known, why I escape*
*in my Xbox and phone.*

*You always remind me of what I've done wrong. I'll soon be 16*
*and I need to move on.*
*They've told you to teach me independence skills, but all that*
*we have are a battle of wills.*
*Are they so stupid that they can't understand, I still feel like a*
*toddler, but my body's a man.*
*Until you have met my early life needs, I cannot move on and I*
*cannot succeed.*

*Pushed down a road that I truly can't face, expected to enter*
*the adulthood race.*
*Getting a job and running a home, perhaps now you know*
*why I hide in my phone.*
*I want to avoid leaving this place, I know I'm a failure and an*
*utter disgrace.*
*How can they put me out in society? Just the mere thought*
*gives way to anxiety.*
*When it all goes wrong, they won't give a shite. I'll be out in*
*the 'system' and you will fight.*
*Now just get out my room*
*And give me my PHONE!*

I don't need you or anyone. I am a man now. I know my brain thinks weird stuff still. I am fed up of everyone looking at me like they are sorry for me. I don't want their pity. I don't want their noses in my business. I am getting out and starting my real life. I only need my phone and my mates. No one else. Especially not YOU! Not even my sisters. They are annoying and boring. I'm getting out of here.

## WHAT'S HAPPENING HERE?

As children move through their teens, their biological clock is ticking away. It is not all about secondary sexual characteristics and a drive to find a partner; it is also about that phase of separation. At this time, young people are driven to assume their own identity – to separate from their parents.

It is like the toddler who explores from the safe base, except that in adolescence the drive to assert an individual personality is so strong that the young person can be actively rejecting (like Rosie in our example above). At the same time, there are unmet needs and confusion about identity for some young people. They may engage in dangerous behaviours or be vulnerable to peer pressure in their drive to belong to a peer group and gain acceptance. They are constantly crying out for help while insisting that you leave them alone. They are grown up now. It is so hard for a traumatised child to assert their own identity, when they are so unsure of their roots. Their unmet needs set little traps for them, keeping them stuck in fear and uncertainty.

This is when young people are vulnerable to the influence of those who will validate their fears but show them a way forward to acceptance, and a way to mask the pain through drugs or alcohol or the adrenaline rush of running with a gang.

# ☿ REMEMBER...

✓ Once a young person enters puberty, they also enter a second phase of neurological development. If their brain was a computer, the analogy would be that the system was clogged, and slow. To work better, it needs a de-fragmentation program and linking to a high-speed system. Effectively, both these things happen, but (as with your computer) during the process, the brain is not functioning well, and two of the most affected areas are impulse control (which is further compromised by peer groups) and communication. The process is typically complete by the age of 25.

✓ The issue with young people who have suffered early trauma is that as their early developmental needs may still remain unmet, they are expressed via immature behaviours and unrealistic expectations. The child struggles to enter the second most important developmental stage of their life with the first still incomplete. As the young adult emerges, we often see a return to home values and a new relationship with parents.

## A FINAL INSIGHT

Just as we encourage our toddlers to take first steps and explore safely, so we need to step back and give our young people room to grow. It is hard. Maybe it is the hardest thing we ever have to do.

Sometimes children can only feel safe enough to start the real attachment process when they have the freedom of control over their own space.

If they know you are there, they will come back in the end.

# 49

# Hope

A common question from parents is: 'Is there any hope?'

It can seem like things will never work out when dealing with entrenched and difficult behaviours. Hope is the only thing that keeps us all going as without hope, what is there?

Hope has seemed to be quite elusive in this long and arduous journey, but suddenly we seem to have a breakthrough moment.

✎ SARAH NAISH: The therapeutic parent's hope

*Hope is sometimes we all have*
*To meet our children's glare.*
*When days are long and nights are fraught,*
*Hope quietly meets us there.*

*When our child has not come home,*
*We hope they are OK,*
*And slamming through the door at night,*
*We hope that they will stay.*

*At darkest times when all seems lost,*
*Search deep within for light,*
*Our children don't know how to ask*
*For help to put things right.*

*Sometimes, a tiny, quiet voice*
*Whispers, 'This will end.*
*Until it does, just keep me close,*
*I am Hope – your constant friend.'*

*And then one day you see reflected*
*In your child's eyes,*
*The hope you nurtured all that time*
*Shining brightly – like a prize.*

*For hope has passed – from you to them,*
*Despite the loss and tears,*
*Your hope for them has now replaced*
*Their hate, your grief, their fears.*

I always had hope. Otherwise, why on earth would I have stuck with it?

As it turned out, my hope was well placed. After Peter left the family (due to having compassion fatigue and being unable to connect to the children), I was resigned to spending the rest of the children's childhoods being a single parent. After six years though, I met Ray. He was literally our 'Ray of sunshine'! After so many years struggling, finally there was help. Ray was open-minded and embarked on a vertical learning curve in therapeutic parenting.

As the years have passed, we encountered more of those little breakthroughs – those tiny, still pauses amidst the chaos when Ray and I just look at each other, smile and squeeze hands. Those smiles say, 'Remember this. Hold this to keep you going in the tough times.'

Now, we have more good days than bad. I see more of the real child than their masking behaviours from trauma. Now it feels like two steps forwards and just the one back.

We are making progress and I can see where we are heading.

## ⟳ MAYBE (Rosie, 17 years)

I've just realised I haven't felt quite as sad, scared and angry as I used to feel.

I remember a time when I couldn't even name my feelings. They just felt like a whirlwind of rage deep in my belly. I was angry all the time and hated it when adults got too close. I still find it a bit tricky but it's getting easier.

When I first came home to Mummy, I called her 'Sarah' for ages. 'Mummy' felt too close for comfort. I couldn't imagine calling her 'Sarah' now. I can even let her hug me sometimes and I actually like it. I'm not telling her that though.

Not long ago, I had a bit of problem with stealing chocolate from the local shop, and after lots of arguments about it Mummy helped me to realise that I was trying to fill a big hole inside me – a hole that she could fill with hugs. She has also helped me to understand that my big scary feelings and tricky moments stem from my history with Jackie and Kevin.

I'm starting to believe that maybe I'm not such a bad kid after all and perhaps not everything is my fault.

Everyone has said that my rudeness has reduced, but it still doesn't take much to push me over the edge. I can talk to Mummy about most things now and if I haven't got the words, she always helps me to make sense of what's happening. Maybe, just maybe. life isn't as bad as I thought it was.

Maybe, just maybe, I have hope.

## WHAT'S HAPPENING HERE?

A little bit of magic. Tiny breakthrough moments for both the parents and the child. We start on our journeys, we realise we have to find a new way. The way Sarah and other parents found was therapeutic parenting.

Over time, little glimmers of hope arrived as the cornerstones of consistency, empathy, naming the need and playfulness created different understanding: a new structure to the brain, a new self-model – for Sarah as well as for Rosie. As therapeutic parents we know we have to go back to the very beginnings, to plug developmental gaps, to create connections, to find joy in each other, but when we are able to, the rewards are unimaginable.

## ♀ REMEMBER...

- ✓ Treasure the moments, make the most of them, use them to create more moments of remembered enjoyment later. Create new memories, a new narrative. You have the power, you are life changers.

# 50

# **Our Family**

All we hope for is to transition the children from their background of trauma, into a position where they can begin to trust their parents, and the parents can trust them! This is most definitely a two-way street.

In this family, the position of mutual trust with a real sense of family stability is almost arrived at by surprise.

✎ SARAH NAISH: Our journey from trauma to trust

When I started my adoption journey 20 years ago, I remember my little fantasies about the two perfect little girls I was going to adopt. I can smile about that now! If someone had told me how it would be, I would not have believed them. If I had known that adopting the children would end my marriage but enable me to find my true soul mate and wonderful therapeutic parent/father for the children, I could never have thought it possible. After all, who would want to start a relationship with a mad single woman living with five traumatised children and five yappy dogs?!

We still have our challenges, but these days we can meet them head on. Usually we have anticipated them and are well prepared. We still have occasions when mad lies surface – for example, someone having a car accident – almost writing off the car – describing it as 'a puncture which was in no way my fault'; or someone walking home through unlit country lanes in the winter at 5 am and saying it was 'quite light'.

Now the four girls live close by. Sophie is 23 and very close as she lives next door with her two dogs! I am so glad I ignored the advice in the early days to rehome my dogs. She has entirely overcome her fears, and now dogs are the centre of her life. We are still working on her being able to rely on us and ask for help.

Rosie is 27 and lives in the same town. She works alongside me in our company and married Dan four years ago. They have a delightful, securely attached little boy, Arthur. Rosie is a fantastic mum and often laughs with me about how Arthur can be quite 'stubborn and controlling'. I have told her I cannot imagine what it must be like to have a child like that!

Arthur looks exactly like William did when he came home to me. Frequently, I find myself with a lump in my throat looking at this beautiful, confident little boy who has had every opportunity, love and security. I see the child that William would have been, and how much he lost. It is wonderful, poignant and bittersweet.

Katie is 25 and has two little girls, Ellie and Grace, and is in a long-term relationship with their father. The girls are also a delight. Ellie, in particular, is very like Katie and Sophie but with that wonderful confidence born from secure parenting.

Ray and I have loved being grandparents and seeing the world afresh through their eyes. Even now, we still find ourselves being surprised that we only have to say something once and the children remember! All those trauma-based behaviours are simply not there. We don't have to double-think everything. We can be spontaneous, joyful, take risks, make last-minute plans – all the things we could not do for such a long time.

Charley is now 20 and also lives locally and works within our therapeutic parenting organisations. She is quick to learn and has recently managed to start living independently. Best of all she demonstrates empathy and insight when working alongside foster parents. Do we still have our challenges? You bet! But they are very few and far between now and I can honestly say that NOTHING fazes us. We are honest with each other and say it how it is.

And William? Well he is now 24 and has struggled the most to live alongside his lump of uncomfortable trauma. He is in a stable, long-term relationship but resists maintaining meaningful relationships with the family. We remind him too much of what he lost. BUT he is still in contact. He came to Rosie's wedding and has met us all again since. Some family events, like the birth of his nieces and nephews, are simply too frightening for him to integrate yet.

The children still argue but there are no more punch-ups. Nowadays, they can withdraw to their own homes. They never ask me to referee.

Most evenings Ray and I are at home. Just listening to the dogs snoring peacefully...apart from the constant 'ping' of the phone:

'Mum, can you have Ellie on Saturday?'

'Mum, did Arthur leave his socks in your car?'

'Mum, can you feed the dogs for me as I'll be back late?'

'Mum, I think there is something wrong with my electric. I definitely put money on the meter.'

And just very occasionally:

'Hi Mum, it's William...'

## ⌂ HOME (Rosie, 27 years)

I can't believe how far we've all come. How far I've come.

My mum is now my best friend. Yes, Mum! I can even call her 'Mum' now! I couldn't before, because that was what I called Jackie when I was little. Now I know what 'Mum' really means.

It's been a long hard road for all of us, but we're all getting there, some of us more quickly than others.

As a wife and mum myself, I can now begin to appreciate how difficult parenting can be, and my child hasn't even suffered trauma!

Mum and Ray have been amazing. They have supported all of us to become the best we can be. They are wonderful grandparents to all the grandchildren and are always at the end of the phone whenever we need them.

I haven't forgotten the little girl I was and I carry her around in my heart, reassuring her and listening if she has a need. Mum taught me to do that.

Sometimes I get a bit wobbly, particularly if one of my sisters is annoying me. That's when I turn to the sugar. It's getting easier though. Everything is getting easier.

Mum doesn't referee and I don't expect her to.

I still feel a bit responsible for them but I'm not their mum. I don't need to parent them anymore. I trust Mum and Ray to do that now.

I have a good job, working alongside Mum and writing the children's books.

I'm organised and reliable. I have empathy for myself and others.

I now know I'm a good person!

I have hope and purpose.

My sisters are doing well, and William is safe. I know he still finds it hard to connect and do the whole family bit, but I also know he'll get there in his own time. I know he will.

The dark days of my early childhood feel far behind me now, and at times it all feels a bit surreal. Did those things really happen? Was it really that bad? Yes, they did; and yes, it was. Thankfully, I came home.

I came home to my mum.

## A FINAL INSIGHT

Amazingly, after all the trials, it's a happy ending. Not a sugar-coated, tied up with a pink ribbon happy ending, because that's not how life is. What we have here is a real-life happy ending work-in-process! This is what families are about: good times and bad; happy times and sad – knowing that you have people who understand you because they were standing with you every step of the way. Being able to look back and share the memories with laughter, and look forward and meet tomorrow with hope – what a gift!

Whatever the construction of your family, whatever is going on with you, whether you live with your children or if you parent from a distance... What a treasure a family is!

Our families may not be perfect but they are *our* families, interwoven from trauma, love, fear, honesty, structure and therapeutic parenting.

We might not be perfect parents, and our children may not be perfect children.

But, as Rosie often says, 'We are now the best versions of ourselves that we could possibly be.'

# Appendix 1

# The Internal Working Model

Our internal working model is the template through which we view ourselves, others and the world in general. To understand the way in which this is developed we need to go back to the basics of a baby's first experiences, remembering that these first experiences are responsible for activating neuronal pathways and making connections in the cortex of the brain.

Our earliest neuronal pathways are co-constructed with our parents. Our senses, our physical movements and our sense of self are encouraged and enhanced within this relationship that has the power to stimulate appropriate areas of the brain through play. These early neuronal pathways form the foundation for the early emotional, social, physical and cognitive areas as parents play with and stimulate the development of their child.

## Healthy attachment cycle

1. The child experiences discomfort. They are cold, wet, lonely, hungry, bored or scared. (The world is, after all, a big unfamiliar place which is confusingly full of multiple sensory stimuli.)

2. The child expresses their discomfort in the only way they can and cries. The child is expressing a survival need which

they are unable to fulfil for themselves. Human babies are completely vulnerable and reliant on others at birth. Their life depends on their caregivers and so discomfort is perceived by their brain as a threat to their existence.

3. The parent/caregiver responds to the baby's distress. The first thing that happens is that the child is picked up and calmed by the co-regulation, physical contact and soothing noises of the caregiver. This is a very empathic response.

4. The parent/caregiver identifies what the issue is and feeds/changes/cuddles/plays with the baby. Both baby and caregiver experience pleasure in their interaction and this is conveyed by tone of voice, eye contact, facial expression, etc.

5. The baby returns to a resting state and processes (unconsciously). A neurological pathway is established with the prefrontal cortex, which records this interaction and forms part of the baby's emerging knowledge and understanding of their own unique experience of the world.

This child is having a wonderful experience of being loved and being found interesting, funny and clever. The parent/caregiver is supporting the child's cognitive development by talking to them (supporting communication and literacy) and by being consistent and having routines (helping pattern recognition, numeracy and understanding of cause and effect). They are supporting the child's emotional development by co-regulating and being emotionally available, social development by gradually increasing the child's exposure to other family members and friends, and physical development by helping the child to exercise their limbs and encouraging them to reach for objects. Children at this stage process in a sensory way, and this will continue to happen until they develop a vocabulary to describe what they see and feel.

Experiences are held 'in the body' and form the basis of the child's early responses. It is easy to see how this early experience, in which adults are generally parenting in a 'good enough'[1] way, leads to a very positive self-image and working model for the child.

## Deficient or unhealthy attachment cycle

1. The child experiences discomfort. They are cold, wet, lonely, hungry, bored or scared. (The world is, after all, a big unfamiliar place which is confusingly full of multiple sensory stimuli.)

2. The child expresses their discomfort in the only way they can and cries. The child is expressing a survival need which they are unable to fulfil for themselves. Human babies are completely vulnerable and reliant on others at birth. Their life depends on their caregivers and so discomfort is perceived by their brain as a threat to their existence.

3. The parent/caregiver fails to soothe and co-regulate, or shows an angry response, or gives an inconsistent response, leading to stress, confusion and fear in the baby.

4. Needs are not met, are inconsistently met, or are inadequately met. The baby does not have the wonderful experience of joyfulness in their parent's/caregiver's presence, and does not have joyfulness mirrored back to them – or this is inconsistent – leading to stress and anxiety.

5. The baby's experience is inconsistent and frequently stressful.

---

1   I use the term 'good enough' because we all make mistakes. In developmental terms this is quite useful, leading to resilient relationships that can withstand disruption.

6. Processing occurs and neurological pathways are established which again inform the baby's emerging sense of themselves, adults and the world.

This child is also having their brain built. Neurological connections are happening. However, the result is different from that in the healthy attachment cycle. This child cannot trust, has to fight for survival and internalises a model that they are very bad indeed – unlovable and worthless. As for adults, they are unpredictable and unreliable at best, or actively hurt the child at worst, confirming the child's ideas that they deserve nothing better. This idea is so strong that being open to other experiences feels uncomfortable and unsafe. The child knows that anything good that happens can't be true, and they fall quickly back into their old patterns of behaviour and distrust. These feelings intensify when they have just had a positive experience.

A person's earliest experiences therefore form the template for how they view themselves, others and the world.

**Summary of the Internal Working Model**

| Positive | Negative |
|---|---|
| Sense of self: valued, important, loved, safe, worthwhile, beautiful, confident | Sense of self: unworthy, unlovable, stupid, worthless, invisible, unsafe, scared |
| Sense of parents/adults: safe, secure, loving, consistent, predictable, reliable, helpful, trustworthy, caring | Sense of parents/adults: scary, unreliable, unpredictable, untrustworthy, cause pain |
| Sense of world: safe, welcoming, fun, exciting | Sense of world: unsafe, terrifying, hostile, need to survive |

# Appendix 2

# Developmental Stages and Awareness

It comes as no surprise that there are many factors which influence how children and young people develop. If we break this down, then we can look more closely at the reasons for the variations we see in individual cases.

As I write this, we are better placed than ever to begin to understand the impact of the environment on the developing child: our understanding of, and research into, neurodevelopment is growing and developing, posing new questions even as original queries are answered.

In 1977, Urie Bronfenbrenner published *The Ecology of Human Development*, whereby the development of an individual is placed at the centre of external influences, from family and friends to community and school, country and global influences. We now know that environmental influences can literally change the way our genes are expressed, with clear implications for health and medical issues including mental health. For instance, children whose mothers were exposed to chronic and severe stress during their pregnancy have been shown to have a higher incidence of psychological and behavioural disorders. This is linked to the toxic effect of stress hormones, and it has been proven that these children are likely to have higher than average levels of stress hormones as well as higher than average numbers of stress hormone receptors. The result is a child who is easily stressed and fearful of change or transitions. Furthermore, research into epigenetics (the way in which the expression of genetic materials is changed in future generations by the environment of the mother) has shown that the alterations to DNA are handed on to subsequent generations.

Where there has been an insufficient, absent or disengaged attachment or another developmental trauma, the individual will be focused on getting their survival needs met. This focus is driven by the primary emotion of fear. The stress created by this will also disrupt the healthy development of the brain. The individual may filter most of their experience via the fear of being able to survive in this hostile environment. It may be hard to connect and engage with others. The individual may have issues with self-esteem as well as finding it hard to trust or maintain a positive outlook. In this case, executive function (higher brain activity controlling impulsivity, enabling analytical thought, mediating responses, and enabling the capacity to be organised and to plan) is largely shut down, or is dependent on information that will feed into adaptive responses based in fear and presenting possibly as anger or withdrawal that will reinforce the fearful outlook of the individual. Resilience, trust and hope may well be alien emotions. This individual is likely to be resistant to, and fearful of, change.

## Cognitive development

There are many learning theories, but it was Jean Piaget (1896–1980) who proposed a timeline of developing cognitive function:

- Sensorimotor (0–2 years)

    o Differentiates self from objects.

    o Achieves object permanence: realises that things continue to exist even when no longer present to the senses.

- Pre-operational (2–7 years)

    ○ Learns to use language and to represent objects by means of images and words.

- Concrete operational (7–11 years)

    ○ Can think logically about objects and events.

- Formal operational (11+ years)

    ○ Can think logically about abstract propositions and test hypotheses systematically.

The issue that I have with this theory, is that these learning milestones do not necessarily occur at the age that has been indicated as the 'norm' but will be dependent on the pattern of the child's developmental process from conception to birth and through early experiences. Trauma, whether this is a result of early attachment history, illness, maternal substance abuse, a genetic condition or medication, will affect this process, with results that are entirely individual.

We can think of cognitive development as a wall, where each level builds upon the previous one:

| | | | | |
|---|---|---|---|---|
| Experimental | Analytical | Non-judgemental | Balanced | Open-minded |
| Interested | Motivated | Questioning | Resilient | |
| Playful | Confident | Exploring | Secure | Growing |
| Engagement | Joyfulness | Trust | Belonging | |
| Safety | Nutrition | Love | Stimulation | Relaxation |

*Developmental wall (Mitchell 2015)*

If some of the foundation is removed, we get a different picture (see below), and the resulting structure is not able to develop – there are too many gaps.

| | Analytical | | Balanced | |
|---|---|---|---|---|
| Interested | | Questioning | | |
| | | | | Growing |
| | Joyfulness | | | |
| | Nutrition | | Stimulation | Relaxation |

*Developmental wall (Mitchell 2015)*

It has been my observation from my own experiences working with children, and from conversations with many parents, that children seek to rebuild their walls – they may actively seek the activity that they need in order to progress, and this may not be age-appropriate. Similarly, children may display behaviours which are confusing – again, it may be useful to look again at the behaviour in order to get an idea of the developmental stage of the child.

If we want to help our children progress, we first need to establish what stage they are at emotionally, socially and cognitively, or whichever of these areas takes priority. When teaching a child new skills, it is useful to remember that with very young children we always give simple clear instructions, we demonstrate, we encourage, we praise, we let the child find their own pace; however, with older children we just expect them to have the experience to understand an instruction and get on with it. Try taking a step back to build practical skills and confidence in learning.

## Key points

- Development follows consistent sequences. This may mean that key stages need to be revisited, especially in emotional and social areas.

- Early attuned relationships and a 'good enough' environment are key developmental issues.

- Although developmental milestones have been established, developmental trauma may delay or arrest development in key areas.

- Cognitive development is also dependent on early experience.

- Early experience of trauma can affect the individual perception of the here and now.

- The human brain is an astonishing thing! It really is never too late to learn – it just may take more time, effort, practice and support.

# Glossary

**ADD (Attention Deficit Disorder)** The child is unable to concentrate or focus. We would link this to intense anxiety and hypervigilance. *ADHD* (see below) is characterised by the child who is unable to keep still either in mind or body. There seems to be no thought before action (impulsivity), or thought before speaking (blurting out information), and a general difficulty with maintaining focus and concentration. Children with ADD and ADHD can be misunderstood, and their restlessness can cause issues at home, at school and in their social lives.

**ADHD (Attention Deficit Hyperactivity Disorder)** Very similar to *ADD*. May be due to an excess of the stress hormone cortisol.

**Amygdala** The 'smoke alarm' of the brain. Recognises potential threats and prepares the body for the fight/flight response. Closely linked to the hippocampus (see below).

**ASD (Autism Spectrum Disorder)** ASD is characterised typically by a failure to engage socially and there is often an underlying component of anxiety. Behaviours expressed can cover a huge range and may include: sensory issues; difficulty with transitions (even moving from home to school, or class to class); resistance to change; adherence to routines and rituals; and focus on specific areas of interest to the exclusion of others in a way that onlookers find obsessive.

**Attachment Disorder** Occurs where there has not been an attuned (see *Attunement* below) adult to form a secure attachment allowing the best possible environment for development of relationships as well as all other developmental areas. This leads to traumatised behaviours.

**Attunement** The process of bonding by becoming extremely receptive (attuned) to another person's needs and having a desire to meet those needs. In the context of this book, it relates to the relationship between an infant or child and an attuned parent/caregiver who is absorbed in meeting the development needs of the newborn and the child.

**Co-regulation** The process by which the attuned caregiver is first distressed by the infant or child's distress, and then is able to soothe and calm the child by their presence, which in turn reduces the parent's/caregiver's own anxiety. Co-regulation is a key factor in the development of trust.

**Developmental Trauma** Delay or damage to the development of a child whether this is cognitive, emotional, social or physical as a result of influences in utero or early life issues such as medical interventions, hospitalisation, neglect or abuse.

**Developmental Window** The optimal time for specific learning to take place – for example, the foundations of cognitive, emotional, social and sensory development take place before a child reaches 3 years old. However, the brain *is* capable of learning new skills and taking on new information throughout life *unless* there is physical brain damage which limits this capability.

**Dyspraxia** Dyspraxia UK (www.dyspraxiauk.com) states that dyspraxia (also known as developmental co-ordination disorder) is a neurological (brain-based) condition which affects co-ordination and perception (vision, hearing, and sense of yourself in space – proprioception). There may be additional developmental issues.

**Fight/Flight or Stress Response** The unconscious response to a threat to survival which is perceived by the central nervous system at a sensory level *before* the person is aware of the danger. It may be triggered by any of the sensory systems. The response to the threat is to produce adrenaline. This dilates the pupils and increases the heart rate, causing blood to be pumped to the lungs where it is re-oxygenated rapidly in preparation for the muscular needs of fighting and running. Blood flow to the brain is decreased and rational thinking is reduced.

**Global Developmental Delay** A condition in which all areas of development – social, emotional, cognitive (and possibly physical) – are affected. This occurs where there has been brain damage due to illness, trauma at birth, or damage sustained *in utero* (see below) as a result of alcohol or substance abuse.

**Hippocampus** The part of the brain concerned with the formation of memories including forming new memories about past experience and explicit memory (verbal memories and memories of facts and episodes).

**In Utero** In the womb.

**Maternal Cortisol** High levels of the stress hormone cortisol in the mother's bloodstream is poisonous to the developing baby and causes them in turn to have abnormally high levels of stress hormone when they are born. This causes anxiety-related conditions and difficulties including managing emotional states.

**Memory Carousel** A term coined by Sarah Naish, this relates to the difficulty that children who have been traumatised have in accessing memory in the form of a timeline or story; instead they sometimes seem to be able to connect to a memory and sometimes are unable to do this. (See Chapter 31, 'Memory'.)

**Neuroception** The ability to understand and process sensation, both internal (interoception – hunger, toilet urge, fullness, discomfort) and external (exteroception – temperature, pressure, pain).

**Neurological** Relating to the functions of the brain.

**Neurological Damage** Damage to the structure of the brain as a result of injury or toxic substances such as alcohol, drugs or cortisol.

**Neurological Development** The process of developing knowledge and understanding of the world and of the self and others based on experiences which cause electrical impulses to activate relevant areas of the brain.

**Object Permanence** An early developmental stage which enables infants to understand that hidden objects do not disappear. This is often mediated by games of hiding and seeking. Children who have been severely neglected may not have assimilated this knowledge, making them very clingy and fearful of separation.

**ODD (Oppositional Defiance Disorder)** Classed as a conduct disorder, 5% of all children between 5 and 16 years of age are diagnosed with this condition. It is characterised by refusing to comply with adult requests; controlling behaviours; aggression and fighting and an inability to self-regulate. The child may find it hard to exhibit empathy and may demonstrate increased levels of risk taking.

**Overwhelm** A feeling that the individual is unable to take in or process any more information, sensations or emotions. In this highly stressed state it is easy to lose control and be subject to a fight/flight response.

**Post Traumatic Stress Disorder** An emotional response to a deeply shocking and disturbing experience. Criteria include: involvement with a life-threatening event involving intense helplessness, fear and horror. Symptoms include: flashbacks; nightmares; perception of being unsafe; hyperarousal; feeling as though traumatic event is happening in the moment; angry and aggressive outbursts.

**Regulation or Self-regulation** The ability to use cognitive areas of the brain to soothe others or to use strategies to soothe yourself. This is a skill which is acquired in the context of an attuned relationship. (See also *Co-regulation* above.)

**Rewiring the Brain** Enabling the development of new ideas and activating new areas of the brain by providing new experiences and new understanding of the past – also known as 'neuroplasticity'.

**Ruptured Attachment** This occurs when a child experiences a disconnection with their parent/caregiver and causes great distress to the child.

**Sensory Processing Disorder** A disruption in development resulting in difficulties processing sensory information such as touch, taste, hearing, sense of self and position in space (proprioception), sense of fullness, hunger, thirst. The brain receives sensory input (touch, taste, hearing, taste and smell) from specialised organs and sensory receptors situated all over the body and processes this information so that the person can respond appropriately to the environment (for example, sensations of heat, cold and pain help us to survive and stay safe). This gives us an ability to explore because we have confidence in our ability to interact with and adapt to the environment. The effects can include hypersensitivity to touch (think of the traumatised child who will only wear certain clothes, or who hates having their teeth cleaned or their hair brushed); taste, hearing and sense of smell: the feeling of integration of body parts – joints and muscle (proprioception) and the ability to co-ordinate balance and movement (vestibular system). This dysregulation affects our emotional regulation and therefore our ability to think rationally.

**Separation Anxiety** The person is terrified by separations as they have not accomplished the idea of object permanence and are fearful that things or people that are out of sight will disappear for ever. Separation anxiety can also be a result of multiple experiences of separations or movements between families.

**Stimulation/Stimulus** An activation of our central nervous system through our senses – stimulation may be visual, tactile, audible, a smell or a taste. Excitement also provides stimulation to the nervous system, activating the same circuits as fear. Overstimulation can easily result in *overwhelm* (see above).

**Stress Hormones** Cortisol and adrenaline can be highly toxic to a baby *in utero* (see above) and cause the fight/flight response to be activated. High levels of stress = high levels of stress hormones = rapid response to stressful situations.

**Transitions** The changes that children have to manage as they move into care and through the system. Each move means a change in rules, expectations, attitudes, environment, school, etc., and even small changes and transitions (e.g. moving from waking to sleep, from play to going out, from home to school) can feel terrifying.

# Bibliography

Axline, V.M. (1964) *Dibs in Search of Self*. New York: Ballantine Books.

Bowlby, J. (1988) *A Secure Base: Parent–Child Attachment and Healthy Human Development*. New York: Basic Books.

Cook O'Toole, J. (2012) *Asperkids*. London: Jessica Kingsley Publishers.

Cozolino, L. (2006) *The Neuroscience of Human Relationships: Healing the Social Brain*. New York: WW Norton & Co.

Gardner, N. (2007) *A Friend Like Henry*. London: Hodder & Stoughton.

Gerhardt, S. (2004) *Why Love Matters*. London: Routledge.

Gerhardt, S. (2010) *The Selfish Society*. London: Simon & Schuster.

Higashida, N. (2014) *The Reason I Jump*. London: Sceptre.

Hughes, D. (2009) *Principles of Attachment-Focused Parenting: Effective Strategies to Care for Children*. New York: WW Norton & Co.

Hughes, D. and Baylin, J. (2012) *Brain Based Parenting: The Neuroscience of Caregiving for Healthy Attachment*. New York: WW Norton & Co.

Keck, G. (2009) *Parenting Adopted Adolescents: Understanding and Appreciating Their Journeys*. Colorado Springs: NavPress.

Luxmoore, N. (2018) *Feeling Like Crap: Young People and the Meaning of Self-Esteem*. London: Jessica Kingsley Publishers.

Morgan, N (2005) Blame My Brain. London: Walker Books.

Naish, S. (2016) *Therapeutic Parenting in a Nutshell: Positives and Pitfalls*. Self published.

Naish, S. (2016) *William Wobbly and the Very Bad Day: A story about when feelings become too big*. London: Jessica Kingsley Publishers.

Post, B. (2009) The Great Behaviour Breakdown. Claremore: Post Institutes.

Post, B. and Forbes, H. (2006) *Beyond Consequences, Logic and Control: A Love-Based Approach to Helping Attachment-Challenged Children With Severe Behaviors*. Colorado: Beyond Consequences Institute LCC.

Seigel, D.J. (2007) *The Mindful Brain in Human Development: Reflection and Attunement in the Cultivation of Well-Being*. New York: WW Norton & Co.

Seigel, D.J. (2016) *Mindsight: Transform Your Brain with the New Science of Kindness*. London: Oneworld Publications.

Seigel, D.J. (2014) *Brainstorm: The Power and Purpose of the Teenage Brain*. London: Scribe Publications.

Seigel, D.J. (2015) *The Developing Mind: How Relationships and the Brain Interact to Shape Who We Are*. London: Guildford Press.

Shell, D. and Becker-Weidman, A. (2005) *Creating Capacity For Attachment: Dyadic Developmental Psychotherapy In The Treatment Of Trauma-attachment Disorders*. Oklahoma: Wood 'N' Barnes.

Verrier, N. (1993) *The Primal Wound: Understanding the adopted child*. Maryland: Gateway Press.

# Index